JAMES MARTIN
sweet

PHOTOGRAPHY BY PETER CASSIDY

QUADRILLE

Publishing director: Sarah Lavelle
Publishing consultant: Jane O'Shea
Creative director: Helen Lewis
Project editor: Charlotte Coleman-Smith
Art direction & design: Gabriella Le Grazie
Photographer: Peter Cassidy
Food preparation and styling: James Martin,
Chris Start, Janet Brinkworth and Dave Birt
Props stylist: Iris Bromet
Production: Vincent Smith, Emily Noto

First published in 2015 by
Quadrille Publishing Limited
Paragon House
52–54 Southwark Street
London SE1 1UN
www.quadrille.co.uk

Quadrille is an imprint of Hardie Grant
www.hardiegrant.com.au

Text © 2015 James Martin
Photography © 2015 Peter Cassidy
Design and layout © 2015 Quadrille Publishing Limited

Cataloguing in Publication Data: a catalogue record for
this book is available from the British Library.

ISBN 978-1-84949-557-8
Printed in China

CONTENTS

INTRODUCTION

In my time, I've been privileged to work in some of the best kitchens in the world, alongside some of the greatest chefs. Don't ask me how, as I'd say it's mostly been down to luck – being in the right place at the right time. But I guess somewhere along the way you have to make your own luck, and of course you still have to produce the goods, as you do in any job.

For me, though, it's not just a job. It's a life, and one that I will always love. Ever since I watched my grandparents making pastry in front of the old telly, rubbing butter into flour by hand, I've wanted to cook; this, I suppose, was when the seed was first planted.

Nowadays, of course, the pastry bench is the place to be, with bake-offs all over the place. But it was a very different scene back in the early 1990s, when a young lad from Yorkshire entered the kitchens of some of the most well-known and well-respected chefs in the country. To say I was bricking it would be an understatement! Aged just 17, I quickly realised that there was going to be no shortcut to the top.

Pastry wasn't really what I had in mind at the time, but fate intervened: the pastry chef went to the loo, never to been seen again. And so after only three days I was on the pastry section, becoming head of it within four months. Back then, no-one wanted to work on the pastry section. To some, it wasn't seen as manly enough, for there was no heat and sweat and fire, but I reckon the real reason was the hours. As a pastry chef, you work longer shifts than anyone in the kitchen: there are early starts for the breakfast stuff, and you can't go home until the last table has ordered dessert. Not that it bothered me. In fact, it made me like it even more. I was on £90 a week, clocking up 115 hours most weeks, and I didn't know any different. What I did soon discover, though, was that when you're working with the best, you absorb everything like a sponge, and so all those hours paid off.

But it's only when you sit down to write a book that you get chance to share all the recipes, tips and advice you've picked up along the way. It's now almost ten years since my first desserts cookbook came out, and I'm really proud that it's still in print and still going strong. I'm especially thrilled when I hear of young chefs using it as a guide to baking and pastry.

With my next desserts book – the one you're holding in your hands – I wanted to take things further, to show how my cooking has evolved and how much I have learnt, and am still learning, from the great chefs I'm lucky enough to meet. The rum baba is a case in point. There are good ones, and there are great ones, but for me the very best rum baba in the UK is Pierre Koffmann's. The recipe I've included in this book is as close as I've got so far, and I reckon it's pretty close. It might even be close enough to save you the train fare to London to eat at his amazing restaurant, The Berkeley. Although, of course, it's still worth making that journey for so many other reasons...

I remember Pierre Koffmann telling me why chefs need to concentrate on the pastry section: not only is it the biggest section in the kitchen, but also it's their dessert, or even just a petit four, which is the last food you taste before you leave the restaurant, so it needs to create a lasting impression.

Whilst I hope most things in here look impressive (and to be honest, it's easier to make a cake look pretty than a duck leg), the taste must always come first. So what you'll find in this book are the 'best of the best' recipes I've found, made up and borrowed, together with some basic recipes at the front and some handy troubleshooting tips at the back. Of course it's not possible to show you everything to do with baking and pastry in one book, but it will point you in the right direction. The rest is up to you!

This is a book I'm extremely proud of, and I've done all I can to make it work on every level – I even insisted on plating every single dish for the photography, which was all done at my house. I hope you enjoy it.

James

BASICS

There are two types of puff pastry: rough puff and classic puff pastry. The difference lies in the way the butter is incorporated. In this classic recipe, a portion of the butter is added to the flour, salt and water to create a dough, which is then 'laminated' with a large block of butter. The idea is to create layers between the butter and the dough. When the butter melts in the oven it produces steam, which is trapped between the layers of pastry, creating the 'puff'. It's very important to keep all the ingredients cold, even the flour. And always use butter, never margarine. You can store puff pastry in the fridge for 3–4 days, and it freezes very well.

Makes 550g

250g plain flour, plus extra for dusting

pinch of fine salt

300g cold unsalted butter (50g cut into cubes, the rest left in a block)

150ml cold water

1 Put the flour and salt on a marble worktop or in a bowl. Add the cubes of butter and rub together with your fingertips to form crumbs. Stir in the cold water and mix to form a soft dough. If using a bowl, tip out onto an unfloured work surface. Pat out into a 2cm-thick rectangle.

2 Put the block of butter between two pieces of silicone paper and bash out with a rolling pin to a 15cm x 10cm rectangle.

3 Dust the worktop with a little flour and roll out the dough to form a rectangle measuring 30cm x 20cm, with the long side facing you.

4 Remove the butter from the paper and place in the centre of the dough. Fold the short side of the dough over the butter, from left to right, then fold the other side over to meet it, covering the butter and brushing off any excess flour. Pinch together the dough at the top and bottom open ends to seal the butter inside, then fold the dough in half lengthways.

5 Turn the dough 90 degrees, then roll out again to a 30cm x 20cm rectangle, again with the long side facing you. Fold one-quarter of the dough across to the centre, from left to right, then fold the other side over to meet it. Fold it in half lengthways, then repeat the whole process one more time, from the point where you turn the dough 90 degrees. Cover and place in the fridge to chill for 1 hour before using. At this stage the dough can also be frozen and used when required. It will keep for 4 weeks in the freezer.

PÂTE BRISÉE

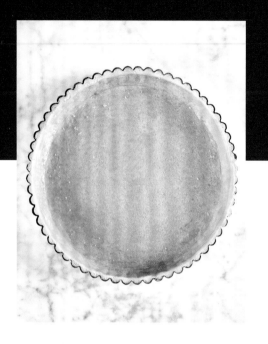

Pâte brisée, or shortcrust, is a great pastry — ideal for most sweet or savoury recipes. You'll need good-quality plain flour and good-quality unsalted butter. The egg prevents the pastry from being too short, and allows you to make tarts and quiches because it stays firm and holds in the tin without cracking. The main thing to remember, as with all pastry-making, is to keep the butter nice and cold so that it mixes into the flour better and, in my opinion, gives a finer pastry. It's also important not to overwork and stretch the dough, as this causes it to shrink dramatically when it's used to line a mould or tin. Always place the dough in the fridge to rest and firm the butter up, which makes it easier to roll out later.

1 Place the flour on a marble worktop or in a bowl, add the butter and salt and rub between your fingertips until the mixture looks a little like coarse breadcrumbs.

2 Make a well in the centre, then crack the egg into the well. Using the tips of your fingers, mix until a sticky dough forms.

3 If using a bowl, tip out onto a floured work surface. Knead lightly until smooth. Flatten until about 1cm thick, then cover with clingfilm and place in the fridge to rest for at least 30 minutes.

Makes 400g

250g plain flour, plus extra for dusting

150g cold butter, diced

1 tsp fine sea salt

1 egg

PÂTE SUCRÉE

This is quite a versatile pastry that freezes very well. In my kitchen it gets used for lining tart tins, but it can be made into biscuits too. My pastry chefs swear by this one. Just be careful not to overwork the dough, and be sparing with the flour when rolling it out.

Makes 500g

275g plain flour, plus extra for dusting

100g cold butter, diced

100g icing sugar, sifted

2 eggs

1 Place the flour on a marble worktop or in a bowl, add the butter and icing sugar and rub between your fingertips until the mixture looks a little like coarse breadcrumbs.

2 Make a well in the centre. Crack the eggs into the well and, using the tips of your fingers, mix until a sticky dough forms.

3 If using a bowl, tip out onto a floured work surface. Knead lightly until smooth. Flatten until about 1cm thick then cover with clingfilm and place in the fridge to rest for at least 30 minutes.

This is great sweet pastry for making things like lemon tart, or when you need to line a mould. It uses a combination of plain flour, cold butter and icing sugar that's been sifted, which means the pastry is very delicate and light. The addition of egg yolks enriches the pastry. I first came across this whilst training as a young pastry chef in the south of France, and it has always been one of my favourite forms of sweet pastry. As always, try not to add too much flour in the rolling-out process. This pastry does need a good hour in the fridge to firm up before using. It also freezes really well.

Makes 550g

250g plain flour, plus extra for dusting

200g cold butter, diced

100g icing sugar, sifted

2 egg yolks

1 Place the flour on a marble worktop or in a bowl, add the butter and icing sugar and rub between your fingertips until the mixture looks a little like coarse breadcrumbs.

2 Make a well in the centre. Add the egg yolks to the well and, using the tips of your fingers, mix until a sticky dough forms.

3 If using a bowl, tip out onto a floured worksurface. Knead lightly until smooth. Flatten until about 1cm thick then cover with clingfilm and place in the fridge to rest for at least an hour.

LINING A TART TIN PROPERLY

Over the thirty-odd years I've been a pastry chef, I've learned a thing or two, including how to line a tart tin properly. The most important thing is to understand how the end product should look. The pastry base should be thin, unshrunken and uncracked. Shrinking and cracking are caused by overworking. If the pastry is bulging, this could be because of a lack of weight during blind-baking. This often happens when baking beans are used. Flour or rice are my preference, but watch you don't undercook the pastry. Really, it's a matter of keeping in mind an image of the finished product and doing everything in sequence to achieve it. Good luck!

soft butter, for greasing

flour, for dusting

pastry, for lining tin

1 egg yolk, beaten, for sealing pastry

1 First, butter the tart tin well using soft butter. I find melted butter tends to sink into the pastry base and can make it soggy.

2 On a lightly floured work surface, roll the chilled, rested pastry to a thickness of about 2mm, turning the pastry 90 degrees every roll. This means you will use less flour to roll it out, which, in turn, means the pastry won't toughen up. Set a small amount of pastry aside for patching up holes later.

3 Carefully roll the pastry onto a rolling pin, then lift it over the tart tin and unroll it, draping the pastry loosely over the case. Don't allow the rolling pin to touch the tin as this will cut the pastry.

4 Gently press the pastry into the base of the tin first, making sure it is reaching all the corners. Draw the rest up and over the sides and press lightly. Be very gentle with the pastry as it can tear if you stretch it. Drape the excess pastry over the sides of the tin so that it hangs down the outside by at least 2–3cm. If there are holes, fill them with the spare pastry.

5 Line the whole tin with a double layer of clingfilm (make sure you use proper clingfilm, not food wrap) then fill with flour, uncooked rice, or dried beans. Gather the clingfilm loosely over the top of the filling then place in the fridge to chill for at least 1 hour. Preheat the oven to 200°C/400°F/Gas mark 6.

6 Put the tart on a baking tray and place in the oven for 15 minutes, then remove from the oven and carefully lift out the clingfilm and filling. Brush the inside of the tart with beaten egg yolk – this will seal any small holes that may have appeared in the tart case.

7 Return to the oven for another 10 minutes, until the pastry is just lightly golden and cooked through. You can reuse the baked flour, rice or beans for blind baking.

8 For a clean finish, use a sharp knife to trim the pastry edges off once the tart case is fully cooked – you can do this with or without the filling.

CHOUX PASTRY ÉCLAIRS

Choux pastry is one of my favourite things to cook. I picked up this recipe whilst working as a pastry chef in a three-star Michelin restaurant in the south of France, and I've used it ever since. Make sure the butter, sugar, salt and water are brought slowly to the boil. If you do this too quickly, the butter will not melt and the water will evaporate. The butter should be diced small so that it melts before you add the flour. To get a really crisp texture, add half a cup of cold water to a preheated tray in the oven before cooking, and then after 20 minutes, open the door for a few seconds to let out the steam.

Makes 12–14 medium éclairs

250ml water

100g cold butter, diced small

1 tsp caster sugar

pinch of salt

150g strong flour

4 eggs

1 Preheat the oven to 180°C/350°F/Gas mark 4 and line a baking sheet with silicone paper.

2 Pour the water into a pan and add the butter, sugar and pinch of salt. Bring to the boil slowly and boil for 1 minute. Add the flour in one go.

3 Cook for a few minutes, beating all the time, until the mixture comes away from the sides of the pan cleanly and is smooth. Tip out onto a silicone-lined tray and leave to cool for 5 minutes.

4 Transfer the cooled mixture to a kitchen mixer or large bowl and beat in the eggs, one at a time, then continue to beat until the mixture is smooth and shiny, about 2 more minutes.

5 Spoon the mixture into a piping bag fitted with a large, plain nozzle, then pipe 10cm-long éclair shapes onto the prepared baking sheet. Smooth out any bumps with the tip of a wet finger. (See also page 38.)

6 Bake in the oven for 25–30 minutes until golden brown and crisp.

7 Remove from the oven and transfer the éclairs from the baking tray to a wire rack to cool.

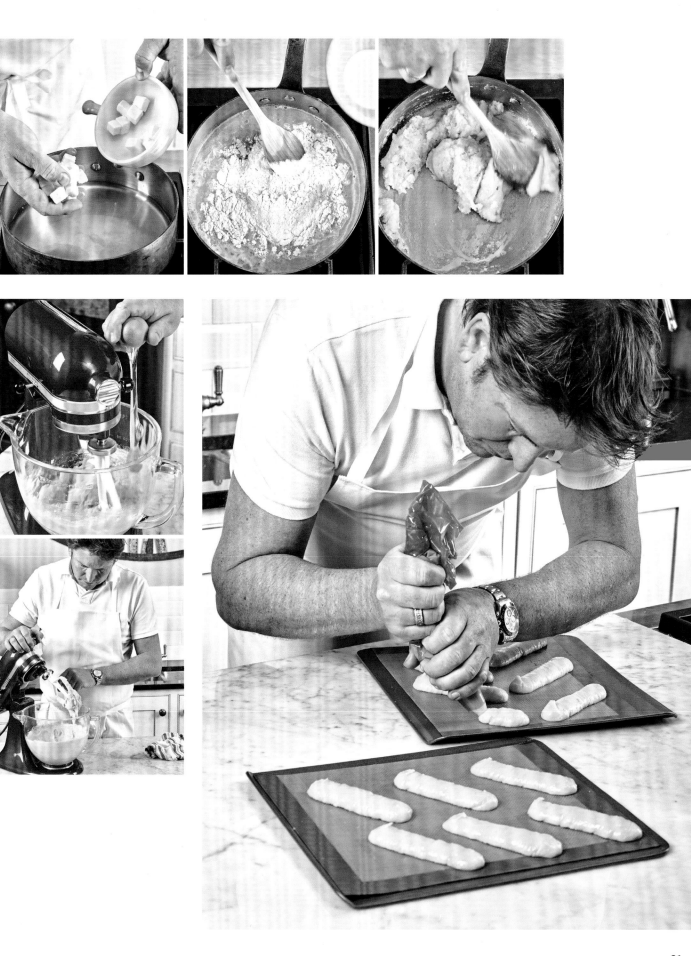

Enriched doughs are actually really simple to make. Once again, it's important to use really good quality ingredients, so do spend that little bit extra on flour and proper butter. My top tip for brioche dough is to use fresh yeast instead of dried. You can buy this from some supermarkets, or your local baker. It's also important to add the softened butter slowly so that you end up with a smooth, but quite sticky, dough. This will stop the baked brioche being dry. If you think of moisture when the brioche goes into the oven, you will get moisture when it comes out!

Makes 800g

50ml room-temperature milk

10g fresh yeast

300g strong flour, plus extra for dusting

10g fine sea salt, plus extra

20g caster sugar

4 eggs

125g softened butter, plus extra
  for greasing

2 egg yolks, for glazing

2 white sugar cubes

1 Whisk the milk and yeast together in a bowl, then set aside for 5 minutes.

2 Put the flour, salt and sugar into a food mixer fitted with a dough hook and mix to combine. Add the yeast mixture and eggs and mix well, scraping the sides down occasionally, until you have a soft, smooth dough. This will take a good 5–6 minutes.

3 Add the softened butter and beat for another 4–5 minutes until it is all incorporated and the dough is soft and shiny. Tip out onto a lightly floured work surface and knead until smooth.

4 Transfer the dough to a clean bowl, cover with clingfilm and leave in a warm place to rise for about 2 hours, until doubled in size, or as recipe specifies. At this stage, you can use the dough for recipes such as Whole Poached Pear Baked in Brioche (see page 103), a plaited loaf or brioche buns.

5 To make brioche buns or a brioche loaf, lightly flour a work surface then tip the dough out onto it and gently knock the air out. Divide the dough between buttered brioche moulds or place in a buttered 23cm x 7cm, 1kg loaf tin. Cover and leave somewhere warm, or at a constant room temperature, to double in size.

6 Preheat the oven to 180°C/350°F/Gas mark 4. Beat the egg yolks with a pinch of salt and brush over the top of the loaf or buns. Crush the sugar cubes over the top. Bake for 25–30 minutes, until golden brown and risen. The loaf or buns should sound hollow when tapped on the bottom.

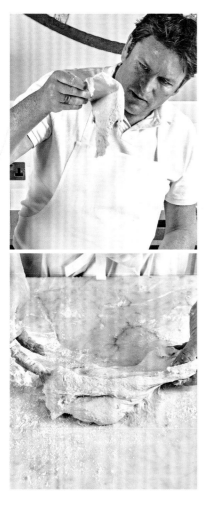

ENRICHED YEAST DOUGH

The method for this dough is similar to brioche, the only difference being that there is a lot less butter, which makes it much easier to work with. While you're adding the butter, the dough will have a glossy finish and still be slightly sticky. Be sure to knead it well at this stage and you'll end up with a lovely, smooth, shiny and pliable dough – the perfect texture for the first prove.

Makes 30-40 small doughnuts

300ml milk

500g strong flour, plus extra for dusting

75g caster sugar

5g table salt

7g fast-action dried yeast,
  or 14g fresh yeast

1 egg, beaten

50g softened butter

1 Warm the milk gently in a saucepan. Mix the flour, sugar, salt and yeast in a kitchen mixer or large bowl until combined, then add the warm milk and egg and mix to a sticky dough.

2 Using the dough hook, knead for about 5 minutes until smooth and elastic. Alternatively, turn out onto a lightly floured work surface and knead for 5 minutes.

3 With the food mixer running, gradually add the softened butter, a little at a time, kneading well in between each addition. It will take about 10 minutes to incorporate the butter and the dough will be sticky. If you're not using a mixer, add the butter to the dough gradually and knead by hand, again for 10 minutes in total.

4 If you're using the mixer, flour the work surface generously and turn the dough out. Now continue to knead lightly until the dough is very pliable, smooth and slightly shiny, but no longer sticky.

5 Place the dough in a large bowl, cover and leave in a warm place to rise for 2 hours, until doubled in size.

6 Mould as required, then cover and leave in a warm place for 1 hour, until doubled in size again, before either baking or deep-frying for doughnuts, or using for a marbled cake (see Banana and Nutella Marbled Cake, page 147).

LAMINATED ENRICHED YEAST DOUGH

This is used for croissants, pains au chocolat and Danish pastries. It contains a lot more butter than enriched dough (page 24), and the butter is incorporated into the dough by lamination, as for puff pastry. This dough contains yeast, which means that it tends to shrink when you start rolling it. Don't despair! Persevere, and press down on the rolling pin so the dough is nice and flat before you add the butter. It's essential to keep the mixture chilled between each turn, otherwise the butter will soften and you'll be tempted to add more flour, causing the dough to shrink. This is why I recommend using a cool marble slab for all doughs and pastries.

Makes 16 croissants
   or 18 Danish pastries

625g strong flour, plus extra for dusting

75g caster sugar

12g fine sea salt

40g fresh yeast

350–400ml cold water

500g butter, chilled

1 egg, plus 1 egg yolk, lightly beaten

1 Place the flour, sugar and salt in a food mixer fitted with a dough hook, or a large mixing bowl. Place the yeast and 50ml of the cold water in a bowl and whisk until the yeast is dissolved. Add to the flour then pour in 300–350ml cold water and mix to a soft dough.

2 Tip out onto a floured work surface and knead really well until the dough feels quite elastic.

3 Roll out the dough to a large rectangle, about 60cm x 30cm, with the long side facing you, then place to one side.

4 Place the chilled butter between two sheets of silicone paper and bash flat with a rolling pin to a 30cm x 20cm rectangle about 1cm thick.

5 Put the butter in the centre of the dough and fold one side of the dough over the butter, from left to right, then fold the other side over to meet it, covering the butter. Pinch together at the top and bottom open ends to seal the butter inside. Fold in half lengthways.

6 Turn 90 degrees then roll out again to a 60cm x 30cm rectangle, with the long side facing you. Fold one-quarter of the dough across to the centre, from left to right, then fold the other side over to meet it. Fold it in half lengthways, then repeat the whole process twice more, starting from the point where you turn the dough by 90 degrees.

7 Fold over, then cover and place in the fridge to rest overnight before using to make croissants or Danish Pastries (see page 184).

CRÈME PÂTISSIÈRE

Crème pâtissière, or pastry cream, is used in fruit tarts, éclairs (see Coffee Éclairs, page 119) and all sorts of other puddings. It is basically a custard made with a thickener; in this case, cornflour. Many recipes use flour, but this can cause the milk in the pan to burn and discolour, affecting the taste. I find cornflour much easier and quicker, and it also helps prevent lumps forming. As the crème pâtissière cools down, dust it with icing sugar before you cover it and put it in the fridge. If you don't, a skin will form and you'll end up with lumps when you stir it.

Makes 750g

500ml full-fat milk

1 vanilla pod, split, seeds scraped out

5 egg yolks

125g caster sugar

50g cornflour

25g butter

icing sugar (optional)

1 Place the milk, vanilla pod and seeds in a saucepan and bring to the boil, then remove from the heat.

2 Whisk the egg yolks and sugar together in a large bowl, then add the cornflour and whisk until smooth.

3 Pour the hot milk over the egg mixture, stirring all the time, then tip back into the saucepan. Cook over a high heat, still stirring all the time, for 2–3 minutes until the mixture has started to thicken.

4 Finally, whisk in the butter, remove from the heat and tip into a clean bowl. Cover with a dusting of icing sugar to stop a skin forming, or place a layer of clingfilm over the surface and chill until needed.

STOCK SYRUP GLAZE

Stock syrup glaze is perfect for brushing over cakes and tarts to give them a lovely, shiny finish. You can add all sorts of flavourings to it (star anise, cinnamon or lemon peel, for example). Just return a little to a pan, add your flavouring and heat through, then leave to infuse for 15 minutes. Strain and use as normal.

Makes 300ml

200g caster sugar

100ml water

1 Heat the sugar and water in a saucepan until the sugar has dissolved. Stir well, then bring to the boil.

2 Remove from the heat and decant into a sealable container. Leave to cool, then cover and store in the fridge until needed (it will keep for up to 2 weeks).

3 To use, brush over the baked cake or tart with a pastry brush and then leave to dry.

CLASSIC MERINGUE

There are three main types of meringue – classic or French, Swiss and Italian. The ingredients don't really change whichever recipe you use; the difference comes with the method. Classic meringue is simply a combination of egg whites and sugar. The key to success is to make sure your bowl and utensils are very clean, free of grease and free of water (free, even, of washing-up liquid!). All of these will cause the whites to collapse. Some cooks prefer to use whites that have been frozen. Over the years, I've found it easier to use fresh ones. You must also be careful not to let any yolk get into the whites before whisking, and always use good-quality caster sugar.

Makes 1 large meringue, or
12 individual meringues

6 egg whites

300g caster sugar

1 Preheat the oven to 110°C/220°F/Gas mark ¼. Line a large baking tray with silicone paper.

2 Make sure your bowl and whisk are very clean, free of grease and completely dry, as any water or grease will affect the meringue.

3 Place the egg whites in the bowl and whisk with a food mixer or an electric whisk on high speed, to soft peaks. Add the sugar, a spoonful at a time, whisking until the mixture is smooth and glossy. You should hear the machine dropping down a gear as it gets to the correct consistency.

4 If you're making one large disc, place the meringue into a piping bag with a 1cm nozzle. Pipe onto the lined baking tray. Alternatively, use 2 tablespoons to space large quenelles (oval shapes) across the tray. Place in the oven for 20 minutes.

5 Turn off the oven and leave for 6–8 hours, or overnight, to dry out. Remove from the oven and cool fully before using.

SWISS MERINGUE

Swiss meringue is a much firmer meringue than its classic cousin, and is ideal as a covering for lemon meringue pies, baked Alaska and ice cream cakes (see Neapolitan Ice Cream Cake, page 78). If you prefer a chewier meringue to a crisp one, this is the recipe to use. The egg whites and sugar are whisked together from the beginning, in a heatproof bowl over a pan of boiling water. A sugar thermometer is essential for this recipe.

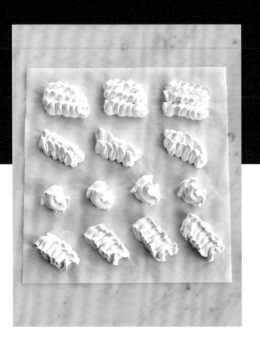

Makes 1 medium meringue,
  or 12 individual meringues

4 egg whites

225g caster sugar

1 Make sure your bowl and whisk are very clean, free of grease and completely dry, as any water or grease will affect the meringue.

2 Place the egg whites and sugar into a large, heatproof bowl set over a pan of simmering water. The bowl should not touch the water. Whisk constantly so the mixture doesn't cook on the bottom, until the sugar has dissolved totally and the mixture has become shiny – this will take about 10 minutes. If you pinch a little between your fingers, it should be silky with no sugar grains. The temperature should be 73°C/163°F – check this with a thermometer.

3 Remove from the heat and continue to whisk with an electric whisk on full speed until the meringue has thickened and has cooled totally. Use the meringue as required.

4 If you're not using the meringue as part of another dish, simply pipe into a large disc or spoon into large quenelles on a silicone-lined baking tray, as for classic meringue (see page 30). Place in the oven for 20 minutes at 110°C/220°F/Gas mark ¼. Turn off the oven and leave for 6–8 hours, or overnight, to dry out. Remove from the oven and cool fully before using.

MACAROONS

I first came across macaroons in St Émilion in the south of France, where they sold them in the little café below my flat. I was a teenager, and working at the nearby Hôtel de Plaisance. I used to go along with my few French francs and buy the macaroons, freshly baked that morning, from the display in the window. It's essential to let the macaroons rest for at least 30 minutes (and up to 90 minutes) before they go in the oven. This allows the mixture to loosen up and results in that lovely smooth crust that's so characteristic. A really good macaroon should also have a soft centre, so be careful not to overcook them!

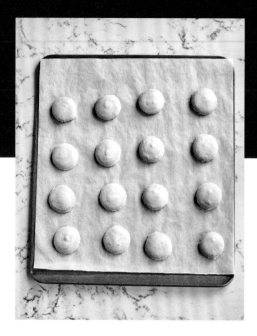

Makes 60 small macaroons

200g ground almonds

200g icing sugar

4 egg whites

100g caster sugar

1   Preheat the oven to 180°C/350°F/Gas mark 4 and line 3 baking sheets with silicone paper. Draw circles on the paper about 30mm in diameter (about the size of a £2 coin) – this is your template for piping. Flip the paper over so the drawings are on the underside.

2   Place the ground almonds and icing sugar in a food processor and blitz to a fine powder. Set aside.

3   Make sure the bowl and whisk you are using for the next step are very clean, free of grease and dry, as any water or grease will affect the meringue. Place the egg whites in the bowl and whisk with a food mixer or an electric whisk on high speed until soft peaks form. Add the caster sugar, whisking until the mixture is smooth and glossy.

4   Pour in the ground-almond mixture and fold in quickly. You almost want to knock the air out of the meringue to end up with a smooth, pipeable mixture.

5   Transfer to a piping bag fitted with a 7mm plain nozzle, and secure the silicone paper to the baking sheets with a dab of the mixture. Pipe discs onto the templates. Set aside for at least 30 minutes until the mixture has spread out slightly.

6   Bake in the oven for 8–10 minutes until crusted and risen. Remove from the oven and leave to cool on the baking sheet.

I wanted to put pastillage into this book mainly because I used to use it so much when I was training as a young pastry chef. I, for one, am not very good at wedding cakes, mainly because I have not got a steady hand for royal icing. With pastillage, you can roll it out, create shapes, then use the firmed-up icing to make whacky and wonderful garnishes for cakes and displays. The edible mouse I've shown here is a variation on the piece I did for my end-of-year college exam. Before you begin, make sure you have plenty of templates and know exactly what you plan to do – pastillage has a habit of drying out even as you use it.

1 Place the gelatine and glucose in a bowl with 50ml cold water for about 5 minutes until the gelatine is softened. Pour into a small saucepan with the lemon juice and heat gently until melted.

2 Sift the icing sugar into a bowl then pour the melted gelatine mixture through a sieve onto it. Mix carefully until it forms a stiff paste the texture of pâte sucrée, then flatten into a 1cm-thick disc. Wrap in clingfilm and place in the fridge for 1 hour to rest or until ready to use. It is important to keep the dough away from air as much as possible as this will start to dry it out.

3 Dust a work surface with an equal combination of cornflour and icing sugar. Remove the dough from the fridge and peel off the clingfilm, then roll it out to a thickness of around 3mm.

4 When you are ready to cut your shapes, make sure the work surface is really clean with no pastillage debris anywhere. Cut into shapes, as desired. Once the shapes and moulds have set, put them aside, uncovered, to dry out fully before using them (this should take about 24 hours).

5 Once you are ready to assemble the parts, or decorate your cake, use royal icing (see page 41) to hold the pieces in place.

Makes 400g

9g powdered gelatine

15g glucose

50ml cold water

2 tsp lemon juice

375g icing sugar, plus extra for dusting

cornflour, for dusting

PIPING

This is a skill that, unfortunately, can only be mastered over time – the more you do it, the better you get at it. I remember the first time I tried to write a name on a cake, I spelt it wrongly, which didn't go down too well with the baker who had spent the night making it! The most important rule is to have everything ready. Don't start anything until you've drawn your templates or planned exactly how and where you are going to pipe the mixture. Here are a few handy tips from someone who does this all the time!

PIPING ÉCLAIRS, PROFITEROLES AND SPONGE FINGERS

I find it best to hold the piping bag at a 45-degree angle to the tray. As you finish piping, simply flick the bag up. This will make a nice clean start and finish. Also, try not to draw the nozzle over the tray, but keep it at a distance, even if it's only just a centimetre or so away, as this will also make the shapes nice and even.

PIPING MACAROONS

First, draw a circular template on silicone paper, then reverse the paper. This will give you the correct size to pipe to, as well as the right amount of mixture, and a good, clean circle. Hold the bag vertically as you pipe.

PIPING DISCS

This may sound weird, but it works: if you're piping a disc (of meringue, say, or biscuit dough), try and move from the hips. Start in the centre and, holding the bag vertically above the tray, swirl the disc from your hips to get a nice Catherine-wheel effect.

PIPING BABY MERINGUES

Hold the bag vertically and pipe a small bulb of meringue onto silicone paper, then sharply, lift directly up and away from the tray. This will give a nice little peak to your meringue.

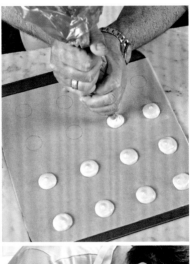

MAKING A PIPING BAG

1 Cut a 30cm x 30cm x 42cm triangle out of silicone paper. Hold it with the longest edge between your hands, point away from you.

2 Twist to form a tight cone. The tip needs to be quite sharp, so maybe twist the paper tighter than you think and the layers of paper shouldn't separate.

3 Fold the top corner of the cone over to secure it in place.

4 Fill with royal icing (see below) and twist the top over to seal. Snip the tip off the end point to give yourself a fine, delicate line. For Danish Pastries (see page 184), pipe in a zig-zag pattern, working quickly. You can also fill the piping bag with melted chocolate, lightly whipped cream or meringue.

ROYAL ICING

Makes 400g

400g icing sugar
2 egg whites
1½ tsp glycerine

1 Sift the icing sugar into a food mixer or large bowl then add the egg whites and beat together until smooth, using a whisk.

2 Add the glycerine and whisk until thickened, rich and very smooth. This process should take 7–10 minutes – it should be thick enough to hold its shape when used to glaze cakes.

3 Use immediately.

It's easy to adapt the basic ice cream recipe by changing just a few ingredients. The more cream or yolks you add, the richer it becomes. This richness is offset by the sugar. However, beware of adding too much. Sugar acts as a defrosting agent, so the more you add, the harder it is for your ice cream to set. The sorbets here are easy to prepare and make a lovely accompaniment to so many dishes. I like to serve them in 'quenelles'. You'll need two spoons for this. Dip one in hot water and take a scoop of sorbet. Mould it into a rugby-ball shape by passing it backwards and forwards between the spoons. Practice makes perfect!

All ice creams and sorbets serve 6–8

250ml milk

250ml double cream

100g caster sugar

1 vanilla pod

4 egg yolks

VANILLA ICE CREAM

1 Place the milk, cream and half the sugar in a saucepan. Using a sharp knife, split the vanilla pod in half lengthways, remove the seeds and add to the milk mixture, together with the pod. Heat until just simmering.

2 Meanwhile, place the remaining caster sugar and the egg yolks in a bowl and whisk them together. Pour the warm milk and cream on to them, whisking all the time.

3 Return the mixture to the saucepan and cook, whisking all the time, until the bubbles start to disappear. Change to a wooden spoon and cook until the mixture thickens just enough to coat the back of the spoon – make sure that you do not boil the mixture. At this point you could use this as a custard (or chill it and use later).

4 Pass the custard through a sieve into a bowl and leave to cool, then place the mixture into an ice cream machine. Churn until the ice cream has set.

5 Once set, transfer the ice cream to a sealable container and freeze until it's needed.

DARK CHOCOLATE ICE CREAM

1 quantity vanilla ice cream (see above)

300g dark chocolate (54% cocoa solids), chopped

1 Follow the vanilla ice cream recipe to the end of step 3, adding the chocolate to the hot custard once it has thickened.

2 Keeping it over a low heat, stir through until smooth and the chocolate has totally melted.

3 Pass through a sieve and churn as normal.

WHITE CHOCOLATE ICE CREAM

1 quantity vanilla ice cream (see page 42), using only 50g caster sugar

300g white chocolate, chopped

1 Follow the vanilla ice cream recipe to the end of step 3, adding the white chocolate to the hot custard once it has thickened.

2 Keeping it over a low heat, stir through until smooth and the chocolate has totally melted.

3 Pass through a sieve and churn as normal.

TOFFEE ICE CREAM

250ml milk
250ml double cream
1 vanilla pod
200g toffees

1 Place the milk and cream in a saucepan. Using a sharp knife, split the vanilla pod in half lengthways, remove the seeds and add to the milk mixture, together with the pod. Heat until just simmering.

2 Add the toffees and leave to melt, stirring occasionally, until smooth.

3 Remove the vanilla pod and churn as normal.

PEANUT BRITTLE ICE CREAM

1 quantity vanilla ice cream (see page 42)
100g smooth peanut butter
200g salted, roasted peanuts
200g caster sugar

1 Follow the vanilla ice cream recipe to the end of step 3.

2 Add the peanut butter to the hot custard and whisk to combine, then churn as normal (no need to sieve).

3 Finely chop the peanuts. Heat the caster sugar in a deep-sided dry frying pan until golden brown and liquid, then tip in the peanuts and stir to combine. Pour the mixture onto a tray lined with silicone paper or baking parchment and leave to set until hard.

4 Break the brittle into small pieces then roughly chop. When the ice cream has churned, spoon the peanut brittle into the machine and churn until the brittle is evenly distributed through the ice cream. Freeze as normal.

STRAWBERRY ICE CREAM

300g strawberries
300ml double cream
140g caster sugar

1 Place the strawberries in a blender and blitz. Add the double cream and caster sugar and pulse until just thickened – you don't want to overwhip the cream.

2 Pour the mixture into an ice cream machine and churn until set. Once it's set, transfer the ice cream to a sealable container and freeze as needed.

SORBETS

Makes 1 litre

500g caster sugar
500ml water

500g crème fraîche
175g caster sugar
75ml water

500g pears, peeled, cored and
  roughly chopped
juice of 1 lemon
50g caster sugar
1 cinnamon stick
400ml cold water
200ml stock syrup (see above)
50ml glucose

500g raspberries or blackberries
200ml stock syrup (see above)
50ml glucose
1 tsp lemon juice
200ml water

500g carrots, peeled and chopped
400ml stock syrup (see above)
400ml water
50ml glucose

500g quinces, peeled, cored and
  roughly chopped
50g caster sugar
1 tsp lemon juice
200ml stock syrup (see page 44)
200ml water
50ml glucose

STOCK SYRUP

Place the sugar and water in a saucepan, stirring briefly just to combine. Bring to a simmer and cook until the sugar has dissolved. Pour into a sealable container and chill until needed.

CRÈME FRAÎCHE SORBET

1 Whisk the crème fraîche, sugar and water together until smooth.

2 Pour into an ice cream machine and churn until frozen. Once set, transfer the sorbet to a sealable container and freeze until needed.

PEAR SORBET

1 Put the pears into a small saucepan with the lemon juice, caster sugar, cinnamon stick and cold water. Bring to the boil, reduce the heat and simmer for 10–15 minutes until completely tender.

2 Strain the pears, reserving the cooking liquor, and place them in a blender. Add the stock syrup, glucose and 200ml of the cooking liquor, then blitz to a fine purée. Pour into an ice cream machine and churn as normal. Once set, transfer the sorbet to a sealable container and freeze until needed.

RASPBERRY OR BLACKBERRY SORBET

1 Purée the raspberries or blackberries, then pass through a fine sieve. You should have about 400ml purée.

2 Combine the purée with all the other ingredients, then transfer to the ice cream machine and churn as normal. Once set, transfer the sorbet to a sealable container and freeze until needed.

CARROT SORBET

1 Poach the carrots gently in the syrup and water for 30 minutes until very soft.

2 Transfer to a blender, add the glucose and blitz to a fine purée. Pass through a fine sieve. Transfer to an ice cream machine and churn as normal. Once set, transfer the sorbet to a sealable container and freeze. until needed.

QUINCE SORBET

1 Put the chopped quinces into a small saucepan with the sugar, lemon juice, stock syrup and water. Bring to the boil, reduce the heat and simmer gently for 30 minutes until totally tender.

2 Place in a blender with the glucose, then blitz to a fine purée. Pour into an ice cream machine and churn for just 10 minutes. Transfer to a sealable container and freeze until needed.

CHOCOLATE DESSERTS

This is a great pudding to place in the centre of the table for everyone to help themselves. Just wait for the reaction when the first spoon hits the bottom of the dish, revealing the rich chocolate sauce that forms as the pudding bakes. Serve with cream or ice cream.

BAKED DOUBLE CHOCOLATE PUDDING

Serves 6

100g melted butter, plus extra
  for greasing

3 eggs

175ml milk

250g self-raising flour

50g cocoa powder

1 tsp baking powder

150g light brown soft sugar

100g dark chocolate drops (70% cocoa
  solids), or dark chocolate, finely
  chopped into approx. 5mm dice

100g milk chocolate drops, or milk
  chocolate, finely chopped into
  approx. 5mm dice

For the sauce

300ml water

200g light brown soft sugar

40g cocoa powder

Preheat the oven to 180°C/350°F/Gas mark 4 and butter a 2-litre ovenproof dish.

Whisk the melted butter, eggs and milk together in a jug until smooth. Sift the flour, cocoa and baking powder into a bowl then stir in the sugar.

Pour the butter mixture onto the flour and mix well to a smooth batter. Stir in the dark and milk chocolate and spoon into the prepared baking dish.

To make the sauce, bring the water and sugar to the boil in a saucepan, then add the cocoa and whisk until smooth. Pour evenly over the top of the batter then place the dish in the oven to bake for 25–30 minutes. The top of the sponge will be just firm to the touch, but underneath there will be a runny chocolate sauce. Serve hot with double cream or ice cream.

Using vegetables in cakes is nothing new, of course, but I really like this combination. Beetroot has a great flavour and a sweetness that softens the bitterness of the chocolate. I've put it just in the filling and the glaze, as I find that adding it to the cake unbalances the recipe.

CHOCOLATE BEETROOT ROULADE
WITH CHOCOLATE CREAM

Serves 8–10

200g dark chocolate (53% cocoa solids), roughly chopped

200g butter

300g packet cooked beetroot, juices reserved, roughly chopped

100g icing sugar

150g cream cheese

5 eggs

175g light brown soft sugar

75g self-raising flour

10 cherries, stalks left on

For the chocolate cream

300ml double cream

200g dark chocolate (53% cocoa solids)

Preheat the oven to 190°C/375°F/Gas mark 5 and line a 23cm x 33cm Swiss roll tin with a sheet of silicone paper.

Put the chocolate and butter in a heatproof bowl set over a pan of simmering (not boiling) water. The bowl should not touch the water. Heat to melt, stirring occasionally, until the chocolate and butter are smooth. Remove from the heat and set aside.

Place the chopped beetroot and juices in a food blender and blitz to a fine purée. Pour all but 125ml of the puréed beetroot into the warm chocolate.

In a separate bowl, beat the icing sugar and cream cheese together until smooth, then beat in 75ml of the puréed beetroot. Set aside with the 50ml puréed beetroot in the fridge while you make the cake.

Whisk the eggs and sugar in a kitchen mixer, or in a large bowl with electric beaters, until very thick and pale in colour. Carefully pour in the cooled chocolate-and-beetroot mixture and whisk until just combined. Sift the flour into the mixture then gently fold in, making sure it has all been incorporated.

Pour into the prepared tin and bake for 10–15 minutes until risen. The sponge should spring back when pressed lightly. Lift the sponge out of the tin and leave to cool slightly.

Meanwhile, heat the cream in a saucepan until just simmering, then remove from the heat and add the chocolate, stirring all the time until the mixture is smooth. Pour into a large bowl to cool. When the mixture is at room temperature, whisk until it just holds its shape.

Spread the chocolate cream over the cooled sponge, leaving a 2cm border around the edge. Score a line 1cm in from one of the longest edges and bend this border over gently. Spoon all but 2 tbsp of the beetroot cream in a line 2cm wide inside the border. Using the silicone paper underneath, roll up the sponge quite tightly, making sure the filling stays inside. Pull the paper towards you as you roll the sponge away from you.

Roll the sponge onto a serving plate – the bottom will be uppermost, giving a smooth finish. Pipe or drizzle over the remaining beetroot cream and puréed beetroot. Finish with a line of cherries down the centre.

I love this dessert. It's often on my restaurant menu, sometimes served with a mild goat's curd ice cream, as the acidity works nicely with the other components. Cakes made with oil have an intriguingly different texture from those made with butter, and the celery leaves add a refreshing note alongside the white chocolate ice cream.

ALMOND AND RAPESEED OIL CAKE WITH POIRE WILLIAM LIQUEUR, CELERY AND WHITE CHOCOLATE ICE CREAM

Serves 4

½ quantity Swiss meringue (see page 32)

2 pears, peeled

1 lemon, halved

100g caster sugar

1 cinnamon stick

25g butter

½ quantity baked Almond and Rapeseed Oil Cake (see page 172)

4 tsp Poire William liqueur

½ quantity White Chocolate Ice Cream (see page 44)

1 handful celery leaves

1 tbsp fennel tops

1 tsp fennel seeds

For the jelly

100ml elderflower cordial

100ml water

2 sheets of gelatine, soaked in cold water for 5 minutes

Preheat the oven to 110°C/220°F/Gas mark ¼, or use a dehydrator set at 63°C. Line a baking sheet, or the tray of the hydrator, with silicone paper.

Spread the meringue to a thickness of about 3mm across the silicone paper. Place in the oven and bake for 2 hours then turn the oven off and leave to dry out. Alternatively, place in the dehydrator for 4 hours.

Meanwhile, make the jelly. Heat the elderflower cordial and water in a saucepan. Add the drained, squeezed gelatine and heat until dissolved. Strain through a fine sieve into a small plastic container and place in the fridge to set for at least 2 hours.

Place the pears in a saucepan with the lemon, sugar, cinnamon stick and enough water to just cover the pears. Bring to the boil, then reduce the heat and simmer for 15 minutes until tender.

Remove the pears from the liquid and allow to cool. Cut in half, remove the core and slice into wedges.

Heat a frying pan until hot, add the butter and pear wedges and sauté for a couple of minutes until golden.

To serve, break the cake apart into small pieces and divide among 4 serving plates. Drizzle with the Poire William liqueur, then place a few pieces of pear next to the pieces of cake. Place a spoonful of the ice cream alongside, together with a few broken pieces of the meringue. Scatter the celery leaves and fennel tops around and finish with a few squares of elderflower jelly and scattering of fennel seeds.

The photos on the previous page show two very different ways of presenting this dessert, using all the same components. In the restaurant we set the Bavarian cream in empty egg shells – if you want to try this at home, you can buy special egg cutters online for a clean finish. The black olive purée needs to be blended to a really smooth paste, to give the final dish the right texture.

WHITE CHOCOLATE BAVARIAN CREAM WITH STRAWBERRIES, CANDIED HAZELNUTS AND BLACK OLIVE PURÉE

Serves 6

150ml milk

4 egg yolks

100g caster sugar

3 gelatine sheets, soaked in cold water for 5 minutes

150g white chocolate, roughly chopped

300ml double cream

2 tbsp demerara sugar

100g wild strawberries

2 figs, cut into small wedges

For the candied hazelnuts

50g icing sugar

100g shelled hazelnuts

For the black olive purée

100g caster sugar

100ml water

100g pitted kalamata olives

Put the milk into a saucepan and bring to the boil. Whisk the egg yolks and caster sugar together until the sugar has dissolved then pour the hot milk onto the eggs, whisking all the time. Return to the saucepan and cook for a couple of minutes until just thickened. Remove from the heat and stir in the drained, squeezed gelatine and white chocolate until both are melted and the custard is smooth.

While the custard is still warm, pass through a fine sieve into a large clean bowl then set aside to cool. Whisk the cream to soft peaks then fold into the cooled chocolate custard. Spoon the Bavarian cream into cleaned egg shells to the very top, or into shallow bowls, and place in the fridge to set for at least an hour. If you're using egg shells, place the filled shells in an empty egg box lined with foil.

Meanwhile, preheat the oven to 180°C/350°F/Gas mark 4. Sieve the icing sugar into a bowl with the hazelnuts and mix to combine. Tip the hazelnuts out onto a baking tray lined with silicone paper and bake in the oven for 5 minutes until crispy. Remove and allow to cool completely.

To make the olive purée, place the sugar, water and olives in a saucepan and bring to the boil. Simmer for 5 minutes then pour into a blender and blitz to a fine purée, leaving the lid open a crack to release the steam.

To serve, sprinkle the demerara sugar over the top of the creams and glaze with a blow torch. You could also place them under a hot grill for a couple of minutes until the sugar has caramelised. If using egg shells, leave the filled eggs in the lined box while grilling.

If you're using egg shells, brush some olive purée in a line across each of 6 flat serving plates. Make a small ring out of Blu Tac or plasticine and place it at one end of the purée. Place the egg shell on top. Dot some strawberries and fig pieces along the purée. Roughly chop the candied hazelnuts and place in between the fruit.

Alternatively, if you're using bowls, lightly glaze the top with a blow torch, then decorate with dots of the purée, in different sizes. Place pieces of strawberry, fig and hazelnuts over the top.

This ganache is best served at room temperature, as the texture is softer and better to eat. If you wanted, you could also use the ganache part of this recipe to make truffles or tart fillings, and of course the salted caramel would go with plenty of other desserts as well.

CHOCOLATE GANACHE
WITH SALTED CARAMEL

Serves 6

For the chocolate ganache

375ml double cream

400g dark chocolate (70% cocoa solids),
  roughly chopped

3 egg yolks

50g icing sugar

For the salted caramel

75g dark brown soft sugar

75g butter

1 tsp fine sea salt

125ml double cream

To serve

50g meringue, crumbled (see page 30)

6 tiny sprigs lemon balm or mint

Strawberry Ice Cream (see page 44)

First of all, make the chocolate ganache. Place 200ml of the double cream in a saucepan and heat until just boiling. Remove from the heat then add the chopped chocolate and whisk until smooth.

Whisk the egg yolks and icing sugar together in a food mixer, or in a large bowl with an electric whisk, until thickened and pale in colour – this will take 5–6 minutes. Pour the chocolate mixture onto the eggs, whisking all the time.

Set aside and allow to cool slightly while you whisk the remaining double cream to soft peaks. When the ganache is cool, fold in the whipped cream, making sure that it's properly combined and no streaks of cream are left.

Line 6 square moulds (each measuring 5.5cm x 5.5cm) with clingfilm. Spoon the ganache into the lined moulds and place in the fridge to chill for 2 hours.

While the chocolate ganache chills, make the salted caramel. Place the sugar and butter in a sauté pan and heat until melted and just caramelising. Add the salt and whisk in the cream, then continue to cook for another 3–5 minutes until thickened. Remove from the heat and allow to cool.

To serve, remove the chocolate ganaches from the fridge 20 minutes before you want to serve them. Turn each one out immediately onto a serving plate.

When the ganache has softened slightly, garnish with the crumbled meringue, a spoonful of salted caramel and sprigs of lemon balm or mint. Serve with a spoonful of Strawberry Ice Cream.

In this adaptation of a dessert from the restaurant menu, rapeseed oil (make sure you use the plain one) gives the ganache a lovely smooth texture. And the blackberry sorbet cuts through the intense richness of the chocolate really well. Simply decorate with a few edible flower petals for a vibrant and sophisticated little dessert.

CHOCOLATE GANACHE WITH BLACKBERRIES AND BLACKBERRY SORBET

Serves 8

For the ganache

280g dark chocolate (70% cocoa solids), roughly chopped

100ml rapeseed oil

50g butter

225ml double cream

For the blackberries

100g blackberries, plus 24 blackberries for garnish

50ml water

50g caster sugar

To serve

75ml double cream, whipped to soft peaks

1 small handful violet flowers

1 quantity Blackberry Sorbet (see page 45)

Melt the chocolate in a heatproof bowl over a pan of simmering (not boiling) water. The bowl should not touch the water. Remove from the heat and cool slightly before beating in the rapeseed oil.

Heat the butter and cream until boiling then remove from the heat and cool to just above room temperature. Whisk into the chocolate mixture. Place eight 7cm x 3cm oval rings or moulds on a baking sheet and pour in the chocolate mixture. Chill for 1–2 hours until set.

Cut the 24 blackberries in half, then set them aside. Place the water and sugar in a saucepan and heat until the sugar has dissolved. Add the remaining blackberries to the pan then pour into a blender and blitz to a purée. Pass through a fine sieve into a bowl and chill until ready to serve.

Take the ganaches out of the fridge 30 minutes before serving and remove the rings. To help do this cleanly, warm each ring very quickly with a blow torch, or dip a cloth into hot water and run it around the ring. Turn one chocolate ganache out onto each serving plate, positioning it slightly off centre.

Spoon dots of purée around the ganache then place 6 blackberry halves onto each plate. Finish with small dots of whipped cream and a few violet flowers and petals. Place a spoonful of Blackberry Sorbet on top of the ganache.

This tasty dacquoise recipe is one I picked up on my travels. Although it works with many styles and types of filling, figs go very well with the hazelnuts in the meringue. I originally made it with poached pears – a great choice when figs are out of season. It's best to make this dessert ahead of time and leave it in the fridge for a few hours, so the meringue softens a little before serving.

CHOCOLATE HAZELNUT DACQUOISE WITH FIGS

Serves 8–10

For the dacquoise

10 egg whites

275g caster sugar

50g cocoa powder

250g ground hazelnuts

For the filling

750ml double cream

1½ tbsp vanilla bean paste

75g icing sugar

10–12 figs

To decorate

twisted willow, or other decorative twigs

sugar spiral (optional)

Preheat the oven to 180°C/350°F/Gas mark 4 and line 2 baking sheets with silicone paper. Draw a 23cm circle on each sheet of paper, then flip them over.

Make sure your bowl and whisk are very clean, free of grease and dry, as any water or grease will affect the meringue.

Place the egg whites in the bowl and whisk with a food mixer or an electric whisk on high speed to soft peaks. Add the sugar, a spoonful at a time, whisking until the mixture is smooth and glossy.

Sift in the cocoa powder and whisk until combined. Fold in the ground hazelnuts, taking care not to knock the air out of the meringue. Spoon into a piping bag fitted with a 1cm plain nozzle. Lift the paper up and pipe 4 blobs on the corner of each tray then press the paper to them to stop it moving.

Pipe concentric rings to fill the circle on each of the lined trays. Next, pipe 6 small discs around the trays (you will have some mixture left over). Bake for 15–20 minutes until golden and just firm to the touch. Transfer to a wire rack to cool completely.

Meanwhile, whisk the cream, vanilla bean paste and icing sugar together until you have firm peaks.

Place one of the meringue discs into a 23cm metal ring on a cake stand or serving plate, trimming it if necessary, then spread a layer of cream 1cm thick on top. Cut 10 figs in half from top to bottom. Place these upright into the cream around the edge of the ring, cut side facing out. Continue all the way around until you have made a border of figs around the edge of the cream. Fold the small discs of meringue into the remaining cream, along with 2 quartered figs. Pile the cream into the centre, pressing it lightly so that it holds the figs in place against the ring.

Place the second meringue disc on top, trimming if necessary, then press down lightly. Lift the ring off the dacquoise. To help you do this cleanly, warm the ring very quickly with a blow torch, or dip a cloth into hot water and run it around the ring.

Decorate with twisted willow and fig wedges, and a sugar spiral, if desired.

This is one of my favourite desserts in the book. It has to be made well, though, starting with the puff pastry. Homemade puff pastry is far better than shop-bought, and as such it really makes this dessert. To get the right finish, bake the pastry between two baking sheets to keep it thin before glazing it with icing sugar. I'm lucky enough to have wild strawberries at the bottom of the garden, but most soft fruit will work with white chocolate.

WHITE CHOCOLATE POT WITH PUFF PASTRY FINGER, WILD STRAWBERRIES AND A WHITE BALSAMIC GLAZE

Serves 6

For the chocolate pots

150g white chocolate, roughly chopped

4 egg yolks

75g caster sugar

100ml double cream

For the puff pastry shards

100g puff pastry (see page 12)

flour, for dusting

1 tbsp icing sugar

For the white balsamic glaze

50ml white balsamic vinegar

2 tsp caster sugar

10g ultratex (see page 188)

To serve

100g wild strawberries and pine berries (or small strawberries)

1 small handful of baby mint sprigs

Start by making the chocolate pots. Melt the chocolate in a heatproof bowl over a pan of simmering (not boiling) water. The bowl should not touch the water.

While the chocolate melts, whisk the egg yolks and sugar together in a food mixer, or in a bowl using an electric whisk, until very thick and pale. Pour the melted chocolate onto the eggs and whisk until incorporated. In a separate bowl, whip the cream to soft peaks, then fold into the chocolate mixture. Pour into 6 small serving pots or ramekins, then place in the fridge until set, at least 2 hours.

Meanwhile, preheat the oven to 200°C/400°F/ Gas mark 6.

Roll the pastry out on a lightly floured work surface to a thickness of about 3mm. Transfer to a baking sheet lined with silicone paper, then place another sheet of silicone paper over the top, followed by another baking sheet the same size. You want the pastry not to rise, so the sheets need to sit snugly, one on top of the other.

Bake in the oven for 12–15 minutes until cooked through and golden brown. Remove and leave to cool between the baking sheets for 5 minutes, then move to a wire rack to cool completely.

Cut the cooked pastry into 6 rectangles measuring 15cm x 2.5cm then dust with the icing sugar. Glaze with a blow torch or under the grill until golden brown.

Heat the white balsamic vinegar and caster sugar in a small saucepan until the sugar has melted, then take off of the heat and whisk in the ultratex. This will thicken the liquid to a gel-like texture. Allow to cool a little before spooning into a small piping bag, then snip off the tip about 3mm from the end.

Place the chocolate pots onto serving plates, then lay one puff pastry shard over the top of each pot. Decorate the pastry with the berries, small sprigs of mint and dots of the white balsamic glaze.

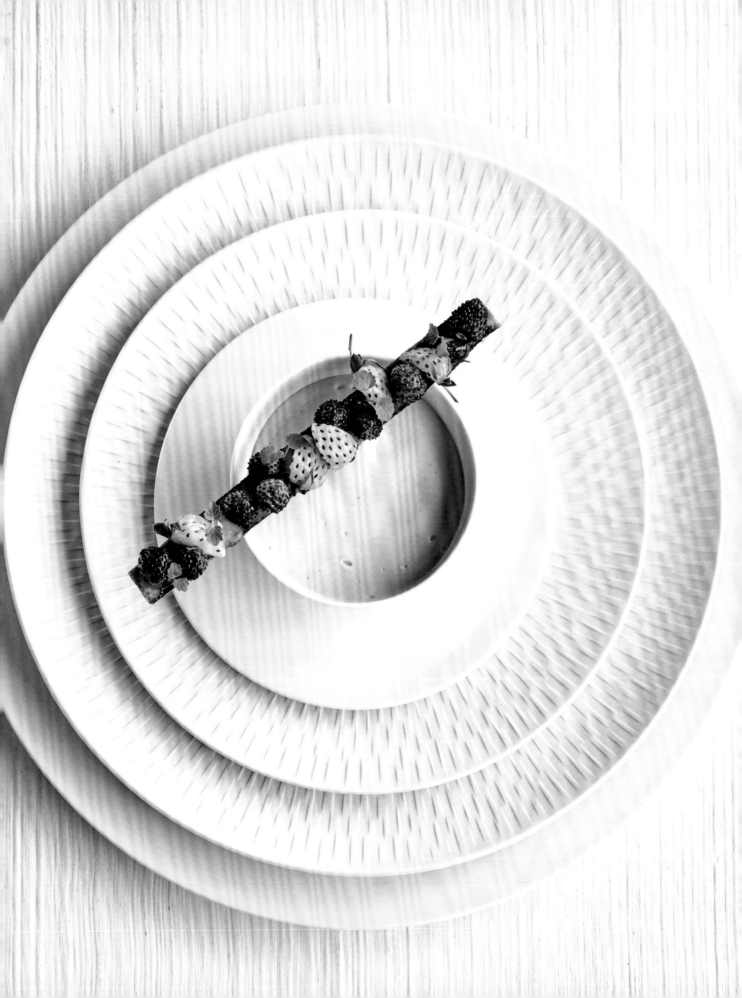

I suppose this is essentially a chocolate fondant, but it is a little lighter than most. Plus I love the flavour of star anise in the chocolate crumb – this is great for sprinkling over ice cream too. You can, of course, freeze the cakes before cooking and then bake them straight from the freezer, giving them 2 minutes longer in the oven. Freeze the banana chunks for the ice cream in a freezer bag.

MELTING CHOCOLATE AND MAPLE SYRUP CAKE WITH CHOCOLATE AND STAR ANISE CRUMB

Serves 4

For the chocolate and maple syrup cake

50g butter

70ml maple syrup, plus extra to garnish

50g dark chocolate (70% cocoa solids), roughly chopped

75g caster sugar

2 eggs

40g plain flour, plus extra for dusting

½ banana, diced

1 tbsp cocoa powder and baby mint leaves

For the chocolate and star anise crumb

75g plain flour

25g cocoa powder, sieved

40g caster sugar

¼ tsp ground star anise

50g cold butter, diced

1 tsp vanilla extract

1 egg yolk

For the banana ice cream

4 bananas, cut into chunks and frozen

¼ tsp vanilla extract

50–75g caster sugar

200–250ml crème fraîche

Preheat the oven to 180°C/350°F/Gas mark 4. Butter and flour 4 metal rings (7cm wide x 5cm high), then place on a baking sheet lined with silicone paper.

Put 40g of the butter and the maple syrup into a saucepan and heat until melted, then add the chocolate and whisk until smooth. Remove from the heat then beat in the sugar, eggs and flour and set aside to cool slightly. Spoon into the rings on the baking tray – they can be chilled at this point until ready to bake.

Meanwhile, make the crumb (shortbread). Place the flour, cocoa powder, sugar and star anise in a bowl and mix to combine. Add the butter and gently rub in until it forms a texture like fine breadcrumbs. Add the vanilla extract and egg yolk and continue to work until the mixture forms a ball.

Press the shortbread mixture onto a silicone-lined baking tray to a thickness of about 5mm. Prick with a fork all over, then bake in the oven for about 15–20 minutes until just firm to the touch. Remove and place the tray on a wire rack until cold.

When ready to serve, place the rings of chocolate cake batter into the oven and bake at 180°C/350°F/Gas mark 4 for 8–10 minutes. They need to still be wobbly in the middle and just cooked around the edges.

While they bake, put the frozen banana chunks into a food processor with the vanilla, half the sugar and half the crème fraîche. Blitz until the bananas start to break down, then add the rest of the crème fraîche and blitz until smooth. Check the sweetness and, if necessary, add the rest of the sugar.

Heat a frying pan until hot and add the remaining 10g butter. When the butter is foaming, add the diced banana and sauté until just golden brown.

When the cakes come out of the oven, dust them with cocoa powder through a small sieve. Press them out of the rings and place one on each serving plate. Crumble some chocolate shortbread next to each cake in a thick line, then spoon the ice cream over this. Garnish with the sautéed banana, baby mint leaves and a drizzle of maple syrup.

CREAM DESSERTS

The secret to a perfect panna cotta lies in having a slight sharpness – here from buttermilk – to balance the sweetness. The consistency is also important: too much gelatine will give you something you could bounce off the kitchen wall; you want to use just enough for the panna cotta to hold its shape when unmoulded. Combined with raspberry jelly, raspberries and warm, sugar-dusted doughnuts, this is a really delicious dessert on the plate. The remaining doughnuts are great with coffee.

BUTTERMILK PANNA COTTA WITH DOUGHNUTS AND RASPBERRY JELLY

Serves 8

250g raspberries, plus 100g for garnish

1 tbsp water

1–2 tsp icing sugar

6 mint sprigs

For the panna cotta

300ml double cream

1 vanilla pod, split and seeds scraped

5 gelatine leaves, soaked in cold water
   for 5 minutes

450ml buttermilk

For the raspberry jelly

50g caster sugar

100ml water

300g raspberries

4 gelatine leaves, soaked in cold water
   for 5 minutes

For the doughnuts

1 quantity enriched yeast dough, made to
   the end of the first prove (see page 24)

vegetable oil, for deep-frying

caster sugar, for dusting

For the mascarpone cream

100g mascarpone cheese

25g caster sugar

50ml double cream

1 vanilla pod, split and seeds scraped

First make the panna cotta. Place the double cream in a small pan with the vanilla pod and seeds, bring to the boil, then remove from the heat. Add the drained, squeezed gelatine and whisk through until dissolved.

Set aside to cool, then add the buttermilk and whisk gently to combine. Carefully pour into 8 small pudding basins or ramekins, making sure you distribute the vanilla seeds equally. Refrigerate for 4 hours, or until set.

For the sauce, place the 250g raspberries, the water and icing sugar in a blender and blitz to a purée. Pass through a fine sieve into a bowl and add more icing sugar if necessary. Chill in the fridge until ready to serve.

For the jelly, bring the sugar and water to a boil in a pan. Add the raspberries and heat until they just start to break down. Remove from the heat and pass through a fine sieve. Don't press, just let the juice drip through.

Measure 300ml juice and return to the saucepan to warm through. Add the drained, squeezed gelatine and stir until completely dissolved. Remove from the heat. Line a shallow baking tray (20cm x 15cm) with clingfilm and pour the jelly over it to a depth of about 3mm. Chill in the fridge until set.

For the doughnuts, divide the dough into 40 equal portions and roll into balls. Line a tray with silicone paper and space the balls evenly across it. Cover with a tea towel. Set aside at room temperature to prove for 20 minutes.

When the dough has proved, heat the oil in a deep-fat fryer to 150°C/320°F. Alternatively, heat the oil in a deep, heavy-based saucepan until a breadcrumb sizzles and turns brown immediately when dropped in. CAUTION: hot oil can be dangerous. Never leave unattended.

Carefully lower the dough balls into the hot oil in batches and deep-fry for 3–4 minutes, until golden. Remove with a slotted spoon and place on kitchen paper to drain. Transfer to a plate and dust generously with the sugar.

For the mascarpone cream, whisk the mascarpone, sugar, cream and vanilla seeds together in a bowl until smooth.

To serve, cut the jelly into squares (about 2.5cm). Briefly dip each panna cotta mould in hot water, then turn out onto a large plate. Place two spoonfuls of the cream on each plate and top with a jelly square. Place two doughnuts on each plate and scatter the remaining raspberries and the mint around. Finish with a drizzle of raspberry sauce.

Once you master this simple meringue roulade, you'll find yourself making it instead of a standard Swiss roll. I've filled it with coffee cream and candied walnuts, but you could also use the candied chestnuts called *marrons glacés* that are often knocking around at Christmas time. With its playful garnish of tuile leaves, this makes a great dinner-party dessert.

COFFEE AND CANDIED WALNUT MERINGUE ROULADE

Serves 10

5 egg whites

275g caster sugar, plus extra for dusting

400ml double cream

10ml Camp coffee essence

1 vanilla pod, split and deseeded

For the tuiles

115g butter, softened

140g icing sugar

3 egg whites

115g plain flour

brown and purple food colouring

gold food spray

For the candied walnuts

150g caster sugar

150ml water

200g walnut halves

vegetable oil, for frying

Preheat the oven to 180°C/350°F/Gas mark 4. Grease a 23cm x 33cm Swiss roll tin and line with silicone paper.

Make sure your bowl and whisk are very clean, free of grease and completely dry, as any grease or water will affect the meringue. Place the egg whites in the bowl and whisk with a food mixer or an electric whisk on high speed until soft peaks form. Add the sugar, a spoonful at a time, whisking until the mixture is smooth and glossy. Spoon into the prepared tin and smooth the surface. Bake for 8 minutes or until golden brown, then lower the oven temperature to 170°C/325°F/Gas mark 3 and bake for 15 minutes or until crisp.

Remove from the oven and turn out of the tin onto a sheet of silicone paper dusted with caster sugar. Remove the paper from the base of the meringue and allow to cool.

For the tuiles, turn the oven up to 200°C/400°F/Gas mark 6. Beat the butter and icing sugar together in a bowl until smooth then whisk in the egg whites, one at a time, until smooth and shiny. Sieve the flour over and fold in gently, then tip half of the batch into a separate bowl. Use the food colouring to colour one batch brown and one purple, then chill in the fridge for 20 minutes.

Place a leaf stencil on a non-stick mat or silicone paper. Using a palette knife, spread the tuile mixture thinly over. Repeat across the mat or paper. Bake for 4–5 minutes, then immediately lay the leaves over the handle of a wooden spoon to curl them. When cold and hardened, spray with edible gold spray.

To make the walnuts, put the sugar and water into a pan and bring to the boil, stirring gently once. Simmer until the sugar has dissolved and the syrup thickened slightly. Add the walnuts and cook for 2–3 minutes. Empty the pan contents onto a sheet of silicone paper.

Pour enough vegetable oil into a sauté pan to cover the bottom by 2cm and heat until just shimmering. Carefully place the walnuts, a few at a time, into the hot oil for a couple of minutes until golden. Drain again on a fresh sheet of silicone paper and leave to cool.

For the filling, whisk the cream, coffee essence and vanilla seeds in a bowl to soft peaks. Spread it over the cooled meringue, then scatter three-quarters of the walnuts over the cream. Starting at the long end, roll up the meringue using the paper to help you.

Decorate the top of the roulade with the tuile leaves and remaining candied walnuts.

With an inexpensive yoghurt maker bought online, making your own yoghurt couldn't be easier. Take my advice and get one. You won't be disappointed – I'm hooked! Here I've used buffalo milk, which is beautifully rich and makes a nice thick yoghurt, but you can use any milk for this lovely, simple dessert.

CHAMOMILE YOGHURT WITH STRAWBERRY COMPÔTE

Serves 4

For the yoghurt

1 litre buffalo milk

2 chamomile tea bags

50g natural yoghurt

1 tbsp clear honey

For the strawberry compôte

40g caster sugar

40ml water

1 chamomile tea bag

200g strawberries, quartered

Bring the milk to the boil in a medium saucepan, then add the chamomile tea bags and swirl around. Leave to infuse for about 30 minutes, or until the temperature of the milk drops just below 50°C/122°F.

Remove the tea bags, squeezing well to give as much flavour to the milk as possible. Whisk in the natural yoghurt, then transfer to a yoghurt maker. Following the manufacturer's instructions, turn the machine on and leave for 6–8 hours.

When the yoghurt has formed, remove from the machine, tip into a sieve set over a bowl and chill in the fridge for 1 hour to firm up, or overnight if you want a texture like thick Greek yoghurt.

Discard the liquid in the bowl, then place the yoghurt from the sieve in a food processor or blender. Add the honey and blitz until smooth. Spoon into serving glasses, then cover and chill until needed.

While the yoghurt chills, make the strawberry compôte. Combine the sugar, water and chamomile tea bag in a small saucepan, bring to the boil and simmer for 1 minute. Remove from the heat, add the strawberries and leave to infuse for 30 minutes.

Spoon the strawberry compôte over the top of the yoghurt to serve.

Parfait is effectively a lighter version of ice cream, aerated with both whisked egg whites and whipped cream before it's frozen, so that it dissolves in the mouth. Make a batch of parfait when you have some time on your hands, then you can keep it in the freezer for up to six months.

ICED LEMONGRASS PARFAIT WITH TOASTED BRIOCHE CRUMBS AND PAN-FRIED MANGO

Serves 8–10

6 stems lemongrass, cut lengthways and bashed lightly

450ml double cream

3 eggs, separated

200g caster sugar

2 slices brioche bread (see page 22, or buy good-quality brioche), roughly chopped

50g butter

1 mango, peeled, cored and sliced

Place the lemongrass and 200ml of the cream in a saucepan. Bring to a simmer then remove from the heat and leave to infuse for at least 30 minutes.

Place the egg yolks and 75g of the sugar in a heatproof bowl set over a pan of simmering water. The bowl should not touch the water. Continue to whisk as the mixture cooks, for about 5–6 minutes, until it has thickened and holds its shape. Remove from the heat, pour the lemongrass-infused cream through a fine sieve onto the mixture and whisk to combine. Continue to whisk until it has cooled.

Take another bowl, making sure it and the whisk are very clean, free of grease and completely dry, as any grease or water will affect the meringue. Whisk the egg whites in the bowl until soft peaks form then whisk in another 75g caster sugar until shiny and the sugar has dissolved. Whisk this into the lemongrass mixture.

Whip the remaining cream to soft peaks and fold in. Line a 1kg loaf tin with clingfilm and pour the mixture in. Tap to settle it, then freeze for 2 hours until just frozen solid.

When ready to serve, blitz the brioche bread in a food processor to fine crumbs. Heat a frying pan until hot, add half the butter and, when foaming, add the crumbs and toast until golden brown. Tip out onto kitchen paper and leave to cool.

Wipe out the pan, then add the remaining butter and sugar. When it's foaming, add the mango and sauté until just golden around the edges.

Slice the parfait and dip one side of each slice into the brioche crumbs. Place the parfait (crumb-side up) onto individual serving plates and lay the mango alongside.

Cambridge cream is similar to a softly set crème brûlée, cooked ever so gently so it just holds its shape. For this dessert, it is burnished to a golden finish with caramelised sugar. The apple granita and purée, both made with Bramley apples, add some welcome tartness, while the hazelnut praline adds crunch and texture.

GLAZED CAMBRIDGE CREAM WITH APPLES AND HAZELNUTS

Serves 4

For the Cambridge cream

5 egg yolks

65g caster sugar, plus extra for glazing

300ml double cream

1 vanilla pod

For the apple granita

1kg Bramley apples

100g caster sugar

1 gelatine leaf, soaked in cold water

For the hazelnut praline

100g caster sugar

25ml water

100g toasted hazelnuts

For the apple purée

500g Bramley apples, peeled, cored and diced

100g caster sugar

¼ vanilla pod

To garnish

2 dessert apples, plus 1 tbsp lemon juice

1 tbsp icing sugar

1 tbsp micro herbs (see page 188)

For the cream, whisk the yolks and sugar in a bowl until light and fluffy. Heat the cream and vanilla pod in a small pan until simmering, then remove from the heat. Leave to infuse for 5 minutes. Pour the cream onto the eggs, mix well then return to the pan. Cook for 10 minutes over a low heat until thick, stirring continuously. It needs to reach 85°C/185°F, at which point it will be thick enough to set. Remove the pod, pour into four 10cm x 4cm rectangular moulds and chill for at least 4 hours.

While the Cambridge cream chills, make the granita. Juice the apples and pour three-quarters of the juice (around 375ml) into a freezable container. Place the rest (around 125ml) in a pan with the caster sugar and heat until dissolved. Add the soaked, squeezed gelatine and heat until dissolved. Pour into the container with the cold apple juice, mixing well. Place in the freezer and freeze for 3 hours, scraping the mixture with a fork occasionally to break up the ice crystals.

To make the hazelnut praline, heat the sugar and water in a frying pan until the sugar melts and turns a rich golden brown. Add the hazelnuts and stir through. Tip onto a silicone-lined tray and leave to cool and set hard. Break into pieces and roughly chop.

To make the apple purée, place the apples, sugar and ¼ vanilla pod in a saucepan, cover and cook for 5 minutes. Stir well, cover again and cook for another 5 minutes until the apples form a purée. Remove the vanilla pod and blitz the purée in a processor or blender. Pass through a fine sieve into a bowl.

For the garnish, peel the apples. Cut one into fine dice and dress with a little lemon juice, then cut the other one with a mandolin into very fine slices. Dust with a little icing sugar and use a blow torch to caramelise.

Sprinkle caster sugar over the Cambridge cream and glaze with a blow torch. Unmould and place to one side of a serving plate. Spoon some apple purée to one side and drag the spoon across the plate, bringing the purée with it. Place a line of chopped praline across the purée, then dress with the apple slices and diced apple. Finish with a scraping of granita and a few micro herbs.

As you can see from the photos on the previous page, this is one impressive-looking cake. The three different ice creams are built up in layers, then encased in Swiss meringue. This is the same meringue used for baked Alaska and lemon meringue pie, which has a good firm texture for piping. Let's face it, who wouldn't like a combination of chocolate, vanilla and strawberry ice cream encased in velvety meringue!

NEAPOLITAN ICE CREAM MERINGUE CAKE

Serves 8–10

1 quantity classic meringue (see page 30)

500ml Strawberry Ice Cream (see page 44), softened

500ml Vanilla Ice Cream (see page 42), softened

500ml Dark Chocolate Ice Cream (see page 42), softened

50g caster sugar

2 quantities Swiss meringue (see page 32)

50g mixed soft fruit

3–4 mint sprigs

Preheat the oven to 110°C/220°F/Gas mark ¼. Line 4 baking trays with silicone paper.

First, make the classic meringue (you may need to do this in batches). Spoon the meringue into a piping bag fitted with a 1cm plain nozzle and pipe a 20cm disc of meringue onto each tray (see also page 38). Flatten the top of the meringue with a palette knife to give a smooth top.

Place in the oven for 20 minutes. Turn off the oven and leave for 6–8 hours, or overnight, to dry out. Remove from the oven and cool fully before using.

Meanwhile, line a 20cm deep-sided cake tin with 2 large sheets of clingfilm, so that they hang out over the sides. Dollop the Strawberry Ice Cream into the tin and spread to the edges so you have a smooth layer of ice cream. Place in the freezer for 30 minutes to firm up, then cover with another layer of clingfilm and repeat with the Vanilla Ice Cream. Return to the freezer for 30 minutes then repeat with the last layer of clingfilm and Chocolate Ice Cream. Place back in the freezer for 30 minutes.

Place one disc of meringue on a large serving plate and remove the Chocolate Ice Cream from the clingfilm. Place the ice cream on top of the meringue. Cover with another disc of meringue, then the Vanilla Ice Cream, another meringue disc and the Strawberry Ice Cream. Finish with the last meringue disc. Wrap in clingfilm and freeze until needed.

To make the spun sugar, heat the caster sugar in a pan until golden brown and liquid all the way through. Set the base of the pan into a bowl or tray of cold water to stop the caramel overheating, then leave for a few minutes until the caramel is slightly more solid. Line a baking tray with a silicone mat and drizzle lines of caramel over it. Leave to harden while you make the Swiss meringue.

Spread half of the meringue all over the top and sides of the gateau. Place the second batch of Swiss meringue into a piping bag fitted with a half-moon nozzle and pipe straight lines up the side of the cake, followed by curls all over the top. Return to the freezer until needed. Garnish with the berries, mint and a few vertical strands of spun sugar.

Some people would say that the stuff that passed for tapioca at school dinners left them scarred for life. But cooked well and treated with care, tapioca is a revelation. In this dessert, its texture makes a great contrast to a smooth and refreshing raspberry soup.

TAPIOCA PUDDING WITH RASPBERRY SOUP

Serves 4

For the raspberry soup

400g raspberries

50g caster sugar

½ lemon, juiced

For the tapioca

50g butter

125g tapioca

125g caster sugar

750ml full-fat milk

150ml clotted cream

1 vanilla pod, split and seeds scraped

100g raspberries

8 tiny mint sprigs

Start by making the raspberry soup. Place the raspberries, sugar and lemon juice in a vacuum-seal pouch or sealable, heatproof bag. Place in a saucepan of water and bring to the boil, then turn the heat off and leave to stand for 10 minutes.

Set a piece of muslin in a fine sieve over a large bowl and open the bag of raspberries into the muslin. Leave to drip through for 4 hours, or overnight if possible. Don't force the raspberries through the sieve — just leave them to drip slowly and you'll have a bright raspberry soup.

Next, make the tapioca. Melt the butter in a heavy-based saucepan or casserole, add the tapioca and stir well so that it's coated in butter. Add 75g of the sugar and keep stirring until it has just melted. Pour in the milk and bring to a simmer, stirring all the time. Add the clotted cream and split vanilla pod and stir well so that everything is combined. Reduce the heat, cover and cook for 20 minutes until the milk is absorbed and the tapioca is tender.

Remove the vanilla pod, then spoon the tapioca into separate serving bowls and sprinkle the rest of the caster sugar over the top. Glaze with a blow torch or under a hot grill, until the sugar has melted and caramelised to a golden brown.

Decorate the top with the raspberries and mint sprigs and serve the raspberry soup in a shot glass alongside.

I love all different types of melon, and I've found it goes really well with honeycomb and a set-cream dessert like cheesecake. Do make sure you reduce the oven temperature so as not to overcook the cheesecakes, or they'll crack. Once they're baked, don't put them in the fridge or they'll become too solid. The best cheesecake I ever tasted was from Eileen's Special Cheesecake in New York. All she sells is cheesecakes – and lots of them! You can buy the honeycomb if you don't want to make it.

MELON AND HONEYCOMB CHEESECAKE

Serves 6

For the honeycomb

200g caster sugar

50ml runny honey

1 tbsp liquid glucose

50ml water

¾ tsp bicarbonate of soda

oil, for greasing

For the cheesecakes

butter, for greasing

60g caster sugar

1 level tbsp cornflour

280g cream cheese

1 egg

½ tsp vanilla bean paste

125ml double cream

For the garnish

¼ watermelon, peeled, juices reserved and cut into balls with a melon baller

¼ each of honeydew, cantaloupe and galia melons, peeled and cut into balls with a melon baller

1 tbsp baby basil cress

Preheat the oven to 150°C/300°F/Gas mark 2 and butter six 5cm metal rings. Line the open bases with proper clingfilm (not food wrap) and place in a deep-sided oven tray.

Start by making the honeycomb. Place the sugar, honey, glucose and water in a saucepan and bring to a boil. Continue to cook until the temperature reaches 160°C/320°F on a sugar thermometer. Remove from the heat and quickly beat in the bicarbonate of soda, stirring constantly.

Grease a baking sheet with a little oil, then line with silicone paper. Pour the honeycomb mixture onto the paper. Set aside until hard, then break into 1cm pieces.

To make the cheesecakes, stir the sugar and cornflour together in a food mixer or large bowl, then beat in the cream cheese. Continue until the mixture is smooth, then add the egg. Add the vanilla bean paste and cream and whisk until smooth, then spoon into the rings, filling them right to the top.

Fill the tray with enough hot water to come 1cm up the side of the rings and place in the oven. Bake for 25 minutes until just set.

Remove the cheesecakes from the oven and cool on a wire rack completely. Once cool, transfer to the fridge for about 30 minutes, or until ready to serve.

While the cheesecakes cool, blitz 50g of the honeycomb in a food processor to fine crumbs and place on a plate.

When you are ready to serve, remove the cheesecakes from the rings. To help you do this cleanly, warm each ring very quickly with a blow torch, or dip a cloth into hot water and run it around the ring. Dip the top side of the cheesecake in the crushed honeycomb to cover it then place, honeycomb-side up, onto the serving plate.

Arrange the balls of melon around each plate. Drizzle with some of the watermelon juices and garnish with pieces of honeycomb and some basil cress.

This is like a French charlotte, really, and is similar to the ones I used to make over there. It's worth having a go at making your own sponge fingers – they're not difficult, and they taste far better than the shop-bought sort. Try not to overwork the bavarois mixture or it might split. It's also a good idea to partially set the bavarois before spooning it into the mould, as it can leak out between the sponge fingers if it's too runny.

RASPBERRY BAVAROIS CHARLOTTE

Serves 6–8

For the sponge fingers

butter, for greasing

4 eggs, separated

70g caster sugar, plus 50g for dusting

35g plain flour

35g cornflour

For the bavarois

150ml milk

½ tsp vanilla bean extract

100g caster sugar

3 egg yolks

6 sheets gelatine, soaked in cold water for 5 minutes

400g raspberries

30g icing sugar

300ml double cream

To garnish

300g raspberries

Preheat the oven to 180°C/350°F/Gas mark 4. Line a baking sheet with silicone paper and grease and line the base and sides of a 17cm deep-sided springform tin.

First make the sponge fingers. Whisk the egg yolks and 35g of the sugar together in a food mixer, or in a bowl with an electric whisk, until light and fluffy. Sift the flour and cornflour onto the mixture and fold in. In another bowl that is clean, free of grease and completely dry, whisk the egg whites until soft peaks form, then whisk in the remaining 35g caster sugar until shiny and the sugar has dissolved. Fold the meringue into the egg-yolk mixture, taking care not to knock out all the air. Spoon into a piping bag fitted with a 7mm plain nozzle and pipe fingers about 8cm long onto the baking sheet (see also page 38). Dust with the extra sugar then bake for 20 minutes until light golden brown and firm to the touch. Remove from the oven and cool on the tray.

While they cool, make the bavarois. Heat the milk and vanilla bean extract in a saucepan until just simmering. Meanwhile, place the caster sugar and egg yolks in a bowl and whisk together, then pour the warm milk over the egg-yolk mixture, whisking all the time. Return the custard mixture to the saucepan and cook until it thickens just enough to coat the back of a spoon – make sure that it doesn't boil. Add the drained, squeezed gelatine to the custard. Stir through until dissolved then set aside to cool in the fridge.

Place the raspberries and icing sugar in a blender and blitz to a purée. Pass through a fine sieve into a bowl. Whip the double cream to soft peaks. When the custard is cool, whisk the purée into it, then fold in the whipped cream. Place in the fridge, whisking every 30 minutes, until it becomes the texture of softly whipped cream and is nearly set.

If the sponge fingers are taller than the prepared tin, trim them to the same height, and trim any uneven edges so that the biscuits sit next to each other snugly. Use them to line the tin by standing them upright, facing outwards and with the trimmed end down. Spoon the bavarois into the centre and chill in the fridge to set for at least 4 hours.

Carefully remove from the tin and transfer to a serving plate. To do this cleanly, warm the ring quickly with a blow torch, or dip a cloth into hot water and run it around the ring. Peel off the paper. Fill the top of the charlotte with tightly packed rings of raspberries.

This looks far more complicated than it actually is, so don't be put off! To create the wood-grain effect of the painter's palette, you need to get your hands on a wood-graining tool, which means a trip to your local DIY shop. Usually used for painting, they are very inexpensive. As an alternative, you could use a pastry brush to make a criss-cross pattern by brushing roughly in opposite directions, although the effect won't be quite so good.

PAINTER'S PALETTE TUILE

Serves 4

½ quantity each of Dark Chocolate Ice Cream (see page 42) and Strawberry Ice Cream (see page 44)

½ quantity each of Carrot Sorbet and Quince Sorbet (see page 45)

For the tuiles

2 tbsp cocoa powder

4 tbsp water

115g butter, softened

140g icing sugar

3 egg whites

115g plain flour

For the sugar brush heads

300g caster sugar

4 tbsp honey, warmed until runny

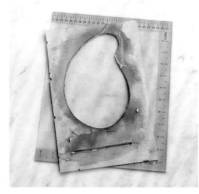

Preheat the oven to 200°C/400°F/Gas mark 6 and line 2 baking sheets with silicone paper.

To make the tuiles, sift the cocoa powder into a wide, shallow bowl and mix to a paste with the water. Using a wood-graining tool, roll it through the cocoa paste straight onto the silicone-lined tray, pressing firmly to create a wood-effect pattern. Repeat until you have quite a thick layer of cocoa all over the silicone paper. Repeat with the second tray, then set both aside to dry for 5 minutes while you make the tuile mixture.

Beat the butter and icing sugar together in a bowl until smooth. Whisk in the egg whites, one at a time, until the mixture is smooth and shiny. Sieve the flour over the top then fold in gently.

Using a large sheet of cardboard, cut the shape of a painter's palette out of the centre (approx. 13cm x 8cm, with a small rectangle 5mm x 12cm alongside; see picture, left). Place the template onto the cocoa-covered baking sheet and spread the tuile mixture over the cut-out palette and rectangle, to a thickness of about 2mm. Carefully remove the template and repeat with the remaining mixture until you have 4 palettes and 4 rectangles (these

are the brush handles). Bake for 5–6 minutes, or until pale golden-brown, then remove and cool on the trays.

While these cool, make the sugar heads for the brushes. Heat the sugar in a pan until golden brown and liquid all the way through. Set the base of the pan into a bowl or tray of cold water to stop the caramel overheating, then leave it there for a few minutes until the caramel is slightly more solid.

Pull a piece of caramel out to make the shape of a long teardrop – this will be the brush head (see picture, opposite). Gently press the tuile handle onto the wider end of the brush head then set aside to cool and harden. Repeat for the remaining brushes.

To serve, place each palette onto a large plate, then brush with the warmed honey until shiny. Top with quenelles or spoonfuls of chocolate ice cream, then carrot sorbet, then strawberry ice cream and, finally, quince sorbet. Set a brush alongside each palette and serve straight away.

Here's a fun and interesting way to turn tuiles into a great dessert. Once you master the art of making these fantastic biscuits, there's no end to what you can create. Just remember that you need to mould them while they are still hot, so make sure you get everything ready when your tuiles are baking in the oven. If you run out of moulding time, try briefly reheating the biscuits in the oven, but you can only get away with doing this once before they'll start to crack when you shape them.

TOFFEE ICE CREAM CONES

Serves 4

½ quantity Toffee Ice Cream
    (see page 44), or whatever
    ice cream you fancy
50g fudge pieces
4 tbsp maple syrup

For the tuiles

115g butter, softened
140g icing sugar
3 egg whites
115g plain flour
50g caster sugar

Preheat the oven to 200°C/400°F/Gas mark 6 and line 2 baking sheets with silicone paper.

For the tuiles, beat the butter and icing sugar together in a bowl until smooth then whisk in the egg whites, one at a time, until smooth and shiny. Sieve the flour over the top then fold in gently.

Take a sheet of cardboard and cut out the shape of a fan with a flat base, about 6cm across the bottom, 16cm across the top and 10cm high. Place the template on the lined baking sheet and, using a palette knife, spread the tuile mixture over it, to a thickness of 2mm. Carefully remove the template. Repeat until you have 4 fans. Place the remaining tuile mixture into a piping bag with a 3mm nozzle and pipe about 5 thin arches along the top of each fan, making sure that the ends overlap onto the fan.

Bake for 2–3 minutes, or until pale golden brown, then remove and cool on the trays for 1 minute. Working quickly, pick up one fan and fold it around to create a cone. Set aside in a short glass to hold it in the fan shape and repeat with the other three. If they set too firmly then place back in the oven for 1 minute to soften and try again. Set aside to firm up.

Make a second template in the shape of a tadpole, to resemble a trail of melting ice cream, with a head approximately 3cm in diameter and a 10cm-long tail. Repeat the process as for the fans, filling the template with the tuile mixture to make 4 'tadpoles'. Bake for 2–3 minutes, then set aside until cold.

Heat the caster sugar in a pan until golden brown and liquid all the way through. Set the base of the pan into a bowl or tray of cold water to stop the caramel overheating, then leave there for a few minutes until the caramel is slightly more solid.

Place a small dot of caramel on a serving plate. Place the head of the 'tadpole' tuile on top and stick a dollop of caramel on top of the head. Quickly place the cone into the caramel and hold for a few seconds until set. Repeat with the remaining caramel and tuiles.

When ready to serve, carefully fill the cones with ice cream, layered with the fudge pieces and maple syrup.

This is a lovely little dessert that uses larger-than-normal macaroons with a combination of walnuts, chocolate and coffee. The candied walnuts are ideal for sprinkling over desserts, but they also make a great bar snack if seasoned with salt and Cajun spices. Be sure to use a good-quality chocolate for the sauce. For a nice shine, add a touch of water to the sauce as it comes together; it may appear to split slightly, but persevere, and once everything is at the same temperature you'll have a lovely rich sauce.

WALNUT MACAROONS
WITH COFFEE CREAM

Serves 6

1 quantity macaroons (see page 34), made with ground walnuts instead of ground almonds

For the candied walnuts

150g caster sugar

150ml water

30 walnut halves

vegetable oil, for frying

For the chocolate sauce

200ml double cream

200g dark chocolate, roughly chopped

50g butter

For the cream filling

450ml double cream

1 tbsp Camp coffee essence

100ml vanilla custard (see page 42)

Preheat the oven to 180°C/350°F/Gas mark 4.

Make the macaroons using 12 circular templates, each one measuring 7cm in diameter. Leave to rest for 30 minutes before baking, then transfer to the oven for 10–15 minutes until golden. Remove from the oven and leave to cool on the tray.

Next make the candied walnuts. Put the sugar and water in a saucepan and bring to the boil. Simmer until the sugar has dissolved and the syrup has thickened slightly. Add the walnut halves and cook for 2–3 minutes. Empty the contents of the pan on to a sheet of silicone paper.

Pour enough vegetable oil into a sauté pan to cover the bottom by 2cm and heat until just shimmering. Carefully place the walnuts, a few at a time, into the hot oil for a couple of minutes until golden brown. Drain again on a fresh sheet of silicone paper and leave to cool slightly.

Make the chocolate sauce. Heat half of the cream, the chocolate and butter in a saucepan until boiling, whisking all the time. Remove from the heat and whisk until smooth then add the remaining cream and whisk once more to combine.

To make the cream filling, whisk the double cream and coffee essence to soft peaks, then whisk in the custard until fully combined and just holding a firm peak. Spread the cream mixture over half the macaroons then sandwich these together with the remaining macaroons.

Spread the chocolate sauce over each serving plate and stand a macaroon upright in the sauce. Repeat with the remaining macaroons, then scatter the candied walnuts around and over them.

FRUIT DESSERTS

This is a wonderfully easy dessert to make, especially if you use good-quality bought filo pastry. Just be careful not to overdo the cinnamon in the filling, as too much will overpower the apple. The cooking time is critical to ensure the outside of the strudel doesn't burn before the inside is cooked through, so if it seems to be browning too quickly, reduce the oven temperature and bake the strudel longer and slower.

SPICED APPLE STRUDEL

Serves 6

For the pastry
butter, for greasing
150g plain flour
2 tsp vegetable oil
20ml white wine vinegar
2–3 tbsp warm water

For the filling
75g melted butter
450g dessert apples
50g caster sugar
1 tsp mixed spice
1 tsp ground cinnamon
75g sultanas

To serve
1–2 tbsp icing sugar
double cream, lightly whipped (optional)

Preheat the oven to 190°C/375°F/Gas mark 5. Grease a baking sheet, then line it with silicone paper.

Place the flour, oil, vinegar and warm water in a food mixer fitted with a dough hook, and mix to a soft dough. Alternatively, place in a large bowl and use your hands. Knead for 10 minutes until the dough is very smooth and elastic. The more you work it, the softer it will get and the easier it will be to roll out thinly. When the dough is really elastic, roll it out over a damp, clean tea towel as thinly as possible into a rectangle ideally about 34cm x 34cm. Brush with some of the melted butter.

Peel the apples, then grate them straight into a bowl, discarding the core. Add the sugar, mixed spice, cinnamon and sultanas and mix to combine. Spread all over the pastry in an even layer then roll up as tightly as possible from the longer end, to form a long sausage.

Transfer to the prepared baking sheet and brush with the rest of the melted butter. Bake for 40–45 minutes until golden brown and crispy. Allow to cool slightly before dusting with the icing sugar. Serve with some lightly whipped double cream, if you like.

There are two types of charlotte: the classically French 'charlotte russe', which is set in a mould; and this English version of apples baked with bread and butter. These are simple flavours that work so well. Served with custard, this is one of the best-tasting desserts you'll ever eat.

BAKED APPLE CHARLOTTE

Serves 6–8

4 Bramley apples, peeled, cored and chopped into 2cm pieces

60g light brown soft sugar

½ tsp ground cinnamon

2 tbsp water

100g softened butter, plus extra for greasing

10 slices soft white bread, crusts removed

2 tbsp demerara sugar

1 Braeburn apple, halved, cored and very finely sliced

Place two-thirds of the chopped Bramley apples in a saucepan with the light brown soft sugar, the cinnamon and water. Cover and cook over a medium heat for 5 minutes. Remove the lid and stir the apples, then cook for another 5 minutes until a chunky purée is formed. Remove from the heat and stir in the remaining apples.

While the apples cool slightly, butter a 17cm-diameter, 10cm-deep pudding basin very well, then butter the bread on one side. Take 7 slices of the bread and cut each one into 2 rectangles the height of the pudding basin. Cut one slice into a disc the same size as the inner base. Cut a disc of silicone or greaseproof paper the same size as the base and arrange the Braeburn apple slices in a fan on the paper. Place this, apple side uppermost, into the base of the pudding basin. Place the small disc of bread on top, buttered side down, then layer in the rectangles around the sides to line the basin, overlapping slightly as you go, buttered sides against the basin.

Spoon the cooled apple mixture into the basin, pressing down lightly. Cut the last two pieces of buttered bread so that they will cover the top. Place them on the top, buttered side up, carefully pressing the edges of the bread down over the edges of the upright pieces of bread, to secure in place. Place a small plate on top of the bread then sit a bag of flour or couple of tins on top to weigh the plate down. Put the whole thing in the fridge for 1 hour.

Preheat the oven to 190°C/375°F/Gas mark 5. Remove the plate and weights from the top, then bake in the oven for 30 minutes until golden brown and crispy. Leave to rest for 5 minutes before turning out onto a plate. Place the plate over the top then carefully turn the basin upside down and tap gently – the charlotte should just slide out. Serve hot with custard or cream.

The idea for this dessert came from one of the chefs at the restaurant, a young nipper of barely 17. I've simplifed it for this book – but if you want to try the original, you'll just have to come along to the restaurant!

CARAMELISED APPLE AND PEAR PUDDING

Serves 4

50g caster sugar

1 tsp vanilla extract

60ml sweet apple cider

1 large apple, peeled, cored and diced

1 large pear, peeled, cored and diced

100g sultanas

175g butter, softened, plus extra
  for greasing

175g light brown soft sugar

3 eggs

175g self-raising flour

½ tsp ground cinnamon

½ tsp vanilla bean paste

For the cream

275ml sweet apple cider

300ml double cream

Butter a 1.2-litre heatproof bowl.

Heat a frying pan until hot, then add the sugar, vanilla and half of the cider. Cook until the sugar becomes liquid and turns a golden caramel colour. Add the diced apple and pear and cook for a couple of minutes until just golden. Pour into the base of the buttered bowl and set aside.

Place the remaining cider in a small pan with the sultanas and warm through, then leave the sultanas to plump up.

Place the butter, sugar, eggs, flour, ground cinnamon and vanilla bean paste in a food mixer or large bowl and beat until light and fluffy, then stir in the sultanas and any remaining cider and spoon carefully into the buttered bowl.

Lay a sheet of silicone paper over a sheet of foil, then make a pleat in the centre with both layers, to create an overlap. Place the sheets over the bowl, foil side up, to form a lid, and secure in place with some string.

Take a long, thin piece of foil and fold in half lengthways to make a handle. Place an upside-down saucer or small plate on a cloth in the bottom of a large saucepan, then half-fill the pan with water. Place the foil-covered bowl onto the long piece of foil, then lift the bowl carefully into the saucepan (the foil acts as a handle later to lift the pudding bowl out of the saucepan). Cover with a lid and bring to a boil, then reduce the heat and simmer for 2 hours.

To make the cream, heat a frying pan until hot, add the cider and cook until reduced by half and slightly thickened. Remove from the heat and cool.

Lightly whisk the cream until soft peaks form then whisk in the cooled cider syrup and continue whisking until it just holds a peak. Serve with the pudding.

This dessert is very close to my heart. I originally made it at college, but reinvented the recipe many years later when I was invited to have lunch with the Queen. This was the dessert that followed a main course of duck from one of Her Majesty's estates. As a boy from Yorkshire who first came to London with little more than a bundle of knives wrapped in a tea towel, this is a very special memory for me, and an experience I will never forget.

SUMMER BERRY FRUIT GRATIN
WITH ALMOND SABAYON

Serves 6–8

3 egg yolks

50g light brown soft sugar

75ml almond milk

4 tbsp honey

25ml amaretto

600g mixed summer berries,
  at room temperature

Preheat the grill to high.

Whisk the egg yolks, sugar, almond milk and honey in a heatproof bowl set over a pan of simmering water until very pale and thickened. The bowl should not touch the water. Make sure the water does not boil, or the yolks will cook too quickly.

Continue whisking for about 6–10 minutes until it's very thick, firm and mousse-like. Add the amaretto and continue to whisk for another 2 minutes. Remove from the heat and set aside to cool slightly.

Place the mixed berries into an ovenproof serving dish. Spoon the sabayon evenly over the berries.

Place the dish under the grill for 2–3 minutes until the top is golden brown and bubbling, then serve immediately.

EᴵᴵR

LE MENU

Croustade d'Oeufs de Caille Nantua

Aiguillettes de Canard Sauvage aux Coings
Sauce au Porto
Haricots Verts aux Tomates Mi-Cuites
Chou Rouge Epicé
Pommes Sablées
Salade

Gratin de Fruits d'Automne
Glacée au Lait d'Amande

LES VINS
Alsace Pinot Gris Tradition "Hugel" 200...
Volnay Taillepieds 1er cru, Domai...
Taylor's Vintage Port 1985

MERCREDI LE 29 OC...

The recipe for blackcurrant délice in my last desserts book went down a storm, so I decided to include a délice in this one too. Passionfruit goes really well with the light texture of a délice. To achieve this lightness, you need to use the right amount of gelatine – just enough to set the mixture, so it remains delicate rather than solid – and line the cake tin with a very thin layer of sponge.

PASSIONFRUIT DÉLICE

Serves 8–10

750ml ready-made mango and passionfruit smoothie

4 eggs, separated

350g caster sugar

4½ gelatine leaves, soaked in cold water for 5 minutes

60ml water

1 ready-made sponge cake or flan case

300ml double cream

For the topping

100ml stock syrup (see page 45)

75ml passionfruit cordial

2½ gelatine leaves, soaked in cold water for 5 minutes

seeds and juice from 1 passionfruit

To decorate

mixed berries

meringue shards

figs

cape gooseberries

lemon verbena leaves

shredded coconut

Place the smoothie in a saucepan and heat until simmering, then cook over a low heat until reduced by about one-third and thickened slightly. Pass through a sieve, reserving the pulp as well as the liquid – you should end up with about 400ml smoothie.

In a bowl, whisk the yolks and 110g of the sugar together until very pale and thickened then pour in the warm smoothie, whisking all the time. Return to the saucepan then bring to a simmer, whisking again until just thickened. Ideally, you want the custard to reach 80°C/175°F to cook the eggs fully.

Remove from the heat then add the soaked, squeezed gelatine and whisk to combine until the gelatine has dissolved. Pass through a fine sieve into a clean bowl then set aside to cool.

Place the remaining 240g sugar and the water in a saucepan and bring to a simmer. Cook until the syrup reaches 121°C/250°F. While the syrup simmers, whisk the egg whites in a large bowl. Make sure your bowl and whisk are very clean, free of grease and completely dry. Whisk until foamy then pour the syrup into the egg whites, whilst continuing to whisk,

until a firm meringue is formed. Continue to whisk on full speed until the meringue has thickened and cooled.

Cut a round from the sponge using a 20cm cake tin as a template, then cut in half horizontally (use the other half for crumbs). Place in the bottom of the cake tin and brush with some pulp from the smoothie.

When the smoothie mix and meringue are cool, whip the cream to soft peaks. Fold the meringue into the smoothie mixture. When it's fully incorporated, fold in the cream. Spoon into the tin, leaving a 5mm gap at the top. Place in the fridge to set for 2 hours.

Heat the syrup and cordial together in a saucepan until hot, then add the soaked, squeezed gelatine and warm through until dissolved. Add the passionfruit and stir through, then set aside to cool. Remove the mousse from the fridge and carefully pour the passionfruit sauce over the top, filling to the top of the tin. Return to the fridge for 30 minutes to set. Decorate with berries, meringue shards, figs, cape gooseberries, lemon verbena and coconut, if liked.

Chefs seem to go through phases with ingredients. Last year was all about passionfruit for me, but at the moment the ingredient I can't get enough of is mango, whether it's tart green mango in savoury dishes or the honeyed sweetness of ripe mango in desserts like this one. With toasted coconut and crumbs from leftover brioche, these clean flavours are like a taste of the Orient.

LIME AND MANGO CREAM WITH TOASTED COCONUT AND BRIOCHE CROUTONS

Serves 4–6

1 mango, peeled, stoned and diced

3 limes

600ml double cream

150g caster sugar

1 slice brioche bread (see page 22), torn into 1–2cm squares

2 tbsp icing sugar

1 tbsp desiccated coconut

Place half the mango in a blender and blitz to a fine purée, then toss half of this with half the remaining diced mango. Divide between 4–6 serving bowls or glasses and set the other half of the mango purée aside. Toss the remaining diced mango with the zest of one of the limes and set aside.

Bring the cream and sugar to the boil in a saucepan. Add the zest and juice of 2 limes and remove from the heat. Whisk well, then pour over the mango in the serving bowls and place in the fridge to set for 3 hours.

Preheat the oven to 180°C/350°F/Gas mark 4.

Toss the brioche and icing sugar together on a baking sheet then bake in the oven for 5 minutes until just golden. Remove from the oven and leave to cool. Transfer the brioche to a plate and set aside.

Put the desiccated coconut onto the same tray and return to the oven for a couple of minutes until golden brown. Tip off the tray into a bowl to cool.

To serve, scatter the brioche croûtons and diced mango over the top of the lime creams. Drizzle with the remaining mango purée then finish with a scattering of toasted coconut.

Microwave sponges have been doing the rounds for a few years now, and they're a great way to make an airy, light-textured cake. Served with a refreshing pear sorbet and a delicate pear jelly, this dessert tastes delicious and looks really pretty on the plate.

PEAR AND POIRE WILLIAM MICROWAVE SPONGE,
PEAR SORBET AND PEAR JELLY

Serves 4

For the pear microwave sponge

4 small pears, peeled, cored and roughly chopped

30g caster sugar

60g hazelnuts

6 egg yolks

30g plain flour

5 egg whites

For the poached pears

200g caster sugar

200ml water

4 small or baby pears, peeled but stem left on

50ml Poire William liqueur, plus extra to serve

5 sheets gelatine, soaked in cold water for 5 minutes

½ quantity Pear Sorbet (see page 45)

To make the sponge, toss the chopped pears with 25g of the caster sugar. Heat a frying pan until hot, then add the pears and cook for 2–3 minutes until caramelised. Remove and set aside to cool.

Place the cooled pears, hazelnuts, yolks and flour in a blender and blitz until smooth, then pass through a fine sieve into a large bowl.

Place the egg whites in another bowl and whisk with a food mixer or an electric whisk on high speed, to soft peaks. Make sure your bowl and whisk are very clean, free of grease and completely dry, as any water or grease will affect the meringue.

Add the last 5g of sugar and whisk until the mixture is smooth and glossy.

Fold the egg whites into the pear batter until fully incorporated. Divide between 4 paper cups or mugs, cover with clingfilm and prick 3 holes in the top. Cook each one separately in the microwave on full power for 2 minutes.

Next, poach the pears. Place the sugar and water in a saucepan, bring to a simmer and cook until the sugar has dissolved. Add the pears and poach gently until just tender, about 10–15 minutes.

Remove the pears and set aside, then add the Poire William liqueur to the poaching liquid and stir through. Add the drained, squeezed gelatine and continue to heat until totally dissolved. Strain through a fine sieve into a small bowl. Transfer to the fridge and leave to set for at least 2 hours.

To serve, place one poached pear on each plate. Place a spoonful of jelly alongside, then break up some pear sponge into chunks and dot around. Drizzle with some Poire William, then finish with a spoonful of Pear Sorbet.

This combination of brioche, poached pear and caramel works brilliantly. Apples would work too, but they must be eating apples, so they'll cook through in the time the brioche takes to bake. Figs are also good in season. Briefly proving the brioche dough just before baking it makes for a lighter result and a contrasting texture to the poached pear. I like a simple caramel sauce with this, but feel free to try it with a salted caramel or chocolate sauce.

WHOLE POACHED PEAR BAKED IN BRIOCHE
WITH CARAMEL SAUCE

Serves 4

For the pear

2 pears with stalk

100ml water

50g caster sugar

juice of 1 lemon

280g brioche dough (see page 22), proved once

flour, for dusting

butter, for greasing

125g natural marzipan, rolled out to 5mm thick

4 bay leaves

For the caramel sauce

100g caster sugar

100g butter

160ml double cream

Preheat the oven to 180°C/350°F/Gas mark 4.

Peel the pears then cut them in half lengthways, splitting the stalk (if this is possible!). Core each half with a teaspoon, then place in a small saucepan with the water, the sugar and lemon juice. Bring to the boil over a medium heat, then cover, remove from the heat and leave to cook through in the residual heat.

Meanwhile, roll out the dough on a lightly floured surface.

Divide the dough into 4 pieces, then form each one into a pear shape, 1cm bigger then the pear halves. Place on a greased tray. Cut the marzipan into pear-shaped pieces the same size as the pears and lay in the centre of the dough.

Remove the pears from the pan and pat dry with kitchen paper. Place these, cut-side down, on top of the marzipan. Gently pull the brioche dough up over the pear.

The dough will shrink back as it cooks. Pull the dough around the stem and stick the bay leaf in at the side of the stem. Set aside to prove for 10 minutes in a warm place.

Bake in the oven for 15 minutes until the dough is cooked through and golden, and the pears are tender.

Meanwhile, make the caramel sauce. Place the sugar in a sauté pan and heat until melted and light golden brown. Whisk in the butter, then add the cream and cook for 3–5 minutes until thickened.

Spoon the caramel over each serving plate, then lay a brioche pear on top.

Pain perdu is really just a fancy version of eggy bread, and this version made with brioche is even fancier. Served with a strawberry compôte, this is equally good eaten for breakfast or as a dessert – the secret is to use strawberries at the height of the season when their flavour is at its peak. A final drizzle of maple syrup adds a lovely mellow sweetness to the strawberries.

STRAWBERRY AND MAPLE SYRUP PAIN PERDU WITH STRAWBERRY COMPÔTE AND CRÈME FRAÎCHE SORBET

Serves 4

For the pain perdu

200ml milk

2 eggs, beaten

25g caster sugar

4 slices brioche bread, each about 2cm thick (see page 22, or use good-quality bought brioche)

25g butter

For the strawberry compôte

350g strawberries, hulled

1 tbsp caster sugar

100ml maple syrup

Crème Fraîche Sorbet (see page 45), to serve

Put the milk, eggs and sugar into a wide, shallow bowl, stir to combine, then add the brioche, 2 slices at a time, and soak on both sides. Place the brioche onto kitchen paper or a clean cloth to drain slightly.

Heat a large frying pan over a medium heat, add the butter and when it's foaming, add the brioche and pan-fry on each side until just golden brown and slightly crispy.

Heat another frying pan until hot, add the strawberries and caster sugar and toss to combine, then sauté for 2–3 minutes until just softened and the juices are running. Allow to cool for a couple of minutes before serving.

Spoon the strawberry compôte into 4 soup bowls, then place a piece of pain perdu in each bowl. Drizzle with the maple syrup and top with a spoonful of sorbet.

Having grown up in Yorkshire, not too far from the so-called 'rhubarb triangle', where some of the world's best rhubarb is grown, I just had to include a rhubarb recipe in the book. This wonderful iced mousse is like a lighter version of ice cream, and the star anise syrup really brings out the flavour of the rhubarb.

ICED RHUBARB MOUSSE WITH GINGER CAKE, STAR ANISE AND CRÈME FRAÎCHE SORBET

Serves 4

For the rhubarb mousse

¼ Swiss meringue (see page 32)

200g rhubarb, trimmed and
   cut into 4cm lengths

50g caster sugar

100ml syrup from a jar of stem ginger

125g full-fat cream cheese

To serve

50g caster sugar

50ml water

1 star anise

100ml vanilla custard (see page 42)

1 slice Ginger and Orange Cake (see
   page 181), or good-quality bought cake

a few slivers of stem ginger

Crème Fraîche Sorbet (see page 45)

1 tbsp citra leaves or baby cress

First, make the Swiss meringue.

Preheat the oven to 200°C/400°F/Gas mark 6.

Reserving a small piece to make twists later, place the rhubarb on a roasting tray and sprinkle over the caster sugar and 50ml of the stem-ginger syrup. Roast in the oven for 10 minutes, or until just tender. Reserve 12 pieces, then transfer the rest to a blender or food processor and blitz to a purée. Set aside to cool.

While the rhubarb cools, whisk the cream cheese and the remaining 50ml stem-ginger syrup in a food mixer, or in a bowl using an electric whisk. When it is very soft, add the rhubarb purée and mix to combine thoroughly.

Fold in the Swiss meringue, making sure it's well mixed in. Line a baking tray with clingfilm, then place 4 small oval-shaped metal rings on top. Spoon the rhubarb mixture into the rings. Place in the freezer and leave to set for at least 2 hours.

Meanwhile, make the star-anise syrup. Place the sugar, water and the star anise in a saucepan, bring to the boil and simmer for 5 minutes. Remove from the heat and leave to infuse.

Spoon some vanilla custard over each serving plate. Break a little of the Ginger Cake into pieces and set these around the plate. Cut the reserved pieces of rhubarb in half lengthways and place on the plate. Add the slivers of stem ginger and carefully peel the reserved rhubarb to make ribbons, then place these on the plate. Carefully lift the ring off each rhubarb mousse. To help you do this cleanly, you can warm the ring very quickly with a blow torch, or dip a cloth into hot water and run it around the ring. Carefully place the mousses over the vanilla custard.

Spoon the star anise syrup over the cake and place a spoonful of Crème Fraîche Sorbet alongside. Finish with some citra leaves or baby cress.

Stem ginger is an invaluable ingredient in so many cakes and desserts. (It also makes a beautifully simple ice cream: just fold sliced stem ginger and some of its syrup through whipped cream and freeze.) Here it's combined with zesty lime curd and striking black and white sesame crisps to make a dessert full of intriguing flavours.

STEM GINGER AND LIME CURD WITH RHUBARB, BLACK AND WHITE SESAME CRISP AND STEM GINGER FOAM

Serves 4

For the rhubarb

200g diced rhubarb

150ml water

25g caster sugar

For the curd

100g curd cheese

juice and zest of 1 lime

100ml syrup from a jar of stem ginger

75ml double cream

For the sesame crisp

125g caster sugar

1 tsp white sesame seeds

1 tsp black sesame seeds

To serve

150ml vanilla custard (see page 42)

2 balls of stem ginger, finely diced

zest of 1 lime

Place the rhubarb, water and sugar in a pan and bring to the boil. Turn the heat off and allow to sit until cool. Divide the rhubarb and juice among 4 serving glasses and chill in the fridge while you make the curd.

Beat the curd cheese until lightened and softened, then stir in the lime zest and juice and 50ml of the ginger syrup. Beat well until properly combined. In a separate bowl, whip the cream to soft peaks, then fold it into the cheese mixture. Spoon over the rhubarb in the 4 glasses and put in the fridge to chill.

Make the sesame crisps while the cheese sets in the fridge. Line 2 baking trays with silicone paper. Place the caster sugar in a dry frying pan and heat until the sugar has melted and turned light golden brown in colour – about 4–5 minutes. Tip out onto one of the lined trays and leave to harden. When the caramel has set hard, break it into pieces and blitz to a fine powder in a food processor.

Preheat the oven to 150°C/300°F/Gas mark 2.

Toast the white sesame seeds for 1 minute in a dry frying pan then tip into a bowl. Repeat with the black sesame seeds, placing them in a separate bowl – this helps you get a more even mix when sprinkling.

Make a template by cutting out a rectangle 2cm x 8cm from the centre of a piece of cardboard or plastic. Place the card on the second lined baking sheet and sprinkle the caramel powder through a fine sieve into the rectangular cut-out – it needs to be about 2–3mm thick. Repeat with the template until you have 8 rectangles spaced across the tray. Sprinkle the sesame seeds over each rectangle. Bake in the oven for 1½–2 minutes until the sugar has melted. Leave on the baking sheet until the crisp has set firm.

Meanwhile, make the custard, adding the remaining stem-ginger syrup once the custard has thickened. Set aside to cool slightly.

To serve, remove the glasses from the fridge and scatter a little diced stem ginger on top of each. Place the ginger custard into an espuma gun, load it with 3 cartridges and squirt the foam on top of the curd in a little pile. Place 2 sesame crisps into the edge of each dessert then finish with a zesting of lime over the top.

I love the sweet, delicate flavour of Sauternes wine, and it's a perfect match with fruit and jelly in this colourful dessert. You could use Champagne instead, if you prefer. A soft set is crucial for this elegant jelly – not like the bouncy sort my mum would make in a rabbit mould. (Sorry, Mum!) I'm tempted to put this on the menu as posh jelly and ice cream... Do you think it will sell?

SAUTERNES AND ORANGE JELLY
WITH STRAWBERRIES

Serves 4

2 oranges

375ml Sauternes

50g caster sugar

5 sheets of gelatine, soaked in
 cold water for 5 minutes

Strawberry Ice Cream (see page 44),
 to serve

100g strawberries

1 handful tagetes or other edible flowers

Cut the peel from the oranges and discard. Use a small, serrated knife to neatly cut the segments out, holding them over a bowl to catch the juices. Put the orange segments to one side.

Heat the Sauternes and sugar together in a saucepan until the sugar has dissolved, then add the drained, squeezed gelatine and heat until it has dissolved, taking care not to whisk too much – you don't want any froth or bubbles.

Remove from the heat and leave to cool for 5 minutes before adding the orange juice. Stir to combine, then pass through a fine sieve into a jug.

Arrange the orange segments over the bottom of 4 soup plates or a large, rimmed cake stand and pour over just enough jelly to cover the base. Chill in the fridge for 30 minutes to set. Pour the rest of the jelly over the top and return to the fridge for 2 hours to set.

When ready to serve, take a blow torch and lightly run over the top of the jelly to create a shiny surface. Top with the Strawberry Ice Cream, then garnish with the strawberries and edible flowers.

Originally inspired by a dessert Michel Roux made on *Saturday Kitchen*, this has become my dinner-party special! I love to spit-roast the pineapple, but baking it in the oven also works really nicely – just keep an eye on it, to make sure the sugar in the maple syrup doesn't start to burn before the pineapple is tender. Take your time and turn down the oven a little if necessary, to allow the spices to 'cook out' and lose their raw taste. This is brilliant served with vanilla ice cream.

STUDDED ROASTED PINEAPPLE

Serves 4–6

1 large ripe pineapple

18 cloves

75g butter

250ml maple syrup

4 star anise

1 cinnamon stick

Preheat the oven to 180°C/350°F/Gas mark 4.

Cut the bottom off the pineapple so that it will stand upright, then peel all the skin away. Stud the pineapple evenly all over with the cloves and place in a roasting tray.

Heat the butter, maple syrup, star anise and cinnamon stick together in a saucepan until the butter has melted, then pour over the pineapple. Place in the oven and roast for 25–30 minutes, basting every 10 minutes or so.

When the pineapple is tender, remove from the oven and glaze with the syrup – it should now be glossy and golden brown.

Cool slightly, then cut into slices to serve and drizzle with the remaining syrup.

PASTRY DESSERTS

I love this simple little dessert that one of my chefs came up with – cherries and chocolate are a great combination. As with any tart, it's vital to make sure the pastry is nice and thin, so you get plenty of filling and not too much pastry. Otherwise it can be more like eating a biscuit!

CHOCOLATE AND CHERRY TART
WITH CRÈME FRAÎCHE SORBET

Serves 8–10

butter, for greasing

1 quantity pâte sucrée (see page 16)

1 egg yolk, for blind-baking

flour, for dusting

400g tin cherries in syrup

400g dark chocolate (minimum 60% cocoa solids), roughly chopped

250ml double cream

100g caster sugar

2 tbsp crushed Hazelnut Praline (see page 75) and edible flowers

1 quantity Crème Fraîche Sorbet (see page 45)

Preheat the oven to 200°C/400°F/Gas mark 6. Butter a 23cm x 4cm loose-bottomed tart tin.

Roll the pâte sucrée out on a lightly floured surface to a thickness of 3mm and use to line the tin. Blind bake the pastry (see page 18).

While the pastry case is baking, drain the cherries through a sieve into a saucepan and place the syrup over a medium heat. Cook the syrup until thick and sticky, and reduced by half. Chop the cherries in half, then add to the pan with the reduced syrup and allow to cool.

Put the chocolate into a large, heatproof bowl. Heat the double cream and sugar together in a saucepan until just simmering then pour over the chocolate and whisk continuously until smooth.

Spread the cherries and their syrup over the base of the tart case, then pour the chocolate filling over the top. Glaze with a blow torch or place under a hot grill until bubbling, then chill in the fridge for at least 30 minutes to set. Remove and leave at room temperature until ready to serve. Place a line of the crushed praline and edible flowers on each plate, then slice the tart and serve with a scoop of Crème Fraîche Sorbet.

Éclairs are a great thing to have in your repertoire – and with my recipe in the Basics chapter, they couldn't be easier. When the times comes to fill them with cream, the trick is that rather than slicing the éclairs open or putting holes in the base, you fill them from the top. This way, the coffee icing seals in the filling, so that when you bite into an éclair, the cream doesn't shoot out of the other end.

COFFEE ÉCLAIRS

Serves 12–14

1 quantity choux pastry éclairs
   (see page 20)

butter, for greasing

For the vanilla cream

1.2 litres double cream

2 vanilla pods, split and seeds removed

For the coffee icing

350g fondant icing sugar

3 tbsp water

2 tbsp Camp coffee essence

Prepare and bake the choux éclairs as described on page 20.

Turn the oven up to 220°C/425°F/Gas mark 7 and grease a baking tray.

For the vanilla cream, pour the cream into a large bowl, add the vanilla seeds and whip to soft peaks.

To make the coffee icing, sift the icing sugar into a large bowl, add the water and coffee essence and whisk together.

Using the tip of a sharp knife, pierce a hole in the rounded end of each éclair. Place the éclairs on their sides and return to the oven for a further 5 minutes so that they become dry and crisp. Remove from the oven and cool on a wire rack.

To serve, transfer the vanilla cream to a piping bag fitted with a 6mm plain nozzle. Pipe the cream into the éclairs through the hole. Dip them into the icing to cover the top evenly. Leave on the wire rack until the icing is set.

This may look elaborate, but once it's broken down into individual elements – from the puff pastry to the basil syrup and pistachio cream – it's actually quite simple. The basil syrup is a great way to incorporate basil into a dessert, and its intense green colour looks fantastic on the plate. Pistachio paste for the pistachio cream is available from specialist food shops and online suppliers.

MILLEFEUILLE OF PISTACHIO AND BASIL CREAM WITH RASPBERRIES

Serves 4

1 quantity puff pastry (see page 12), or good-quality, bought all-butter puff pastry

flour, for dusting

50g caster sugar

450g raspberries

1 tbsp chopped pistachio nuts

4 sprigs basil

For the pistachio cream

50ml warm crème pâtissière (see page 28)

150g caster sugar

75ml water

leaves from 1 large bunch basil

15g pistachio paste

100ml double cream

Preheat the oven to 180°C/350°F/Gas mark 4 and line a baking sheet with silicone paper.

Roll out the pastry on a lightly floured surface to a thickness of 3mm and place on the baking sheet. Place another sheet of silicone paper over the top followed by another baking sheet so the pastry is sandwiched between the trays. Bake in the oven for 15 minutes until golden brown and cooked through. Lift the top tray off and return to the oven for another 5 minutes to crisp up. Set aside on a wire rack to cool.

Meanwhile, make the pistachio cream. Prepare the crème pâtissière. Place the sugar and water in a saucepan and bring to the boil. Add the basil leaves and blanch for 20 seconds. Tip straight into a blender and blitz to a fine purée, then pass through a fine sieve into a bowl. Set aside 2 tablespoons of the basil syrup.

Add the pistachio paste to the remaining basil syrup and whisk, then whisk in the warm crème pâtissière and double cream until it just holds its shape. When ready to serve, transfer to a piping bag fitted with a 5mm nozzle.

When the pastry is cold, cut into 12 small rectangles 2.5cm wide by 12cm long. Dust the rectangles with caster sugar then caramelise with a blow torch or under a hot grill until just golden brown.

Place 1 rectangle onto each of 4 serving plates. Pipe the pistachio cream onto the pastry then top with raspberries. Place a second piece of pastry on top of the raspberries, then repeat with another layer of cream and raspberries. Finish with another rectangle of pastry then garnish with a few raspberries and chopped pistachios. Drizzle over a little of the reserved basil syrup and finish with a few sprigs of basil.

A classic dessert first invented in 1910, in honour of the Paris–Brest–Paris cycle race, this has since become popular all over the world. Sadly, we don't often see it in restaurants nowadays, but it's widely available in patisseries across France and in the UK. With a praline mousseline filling and choux pastry, its simple, precise flavours make it a winner every single time. I've topped mine with a little bit of caramel and flaked almonds to add some texture, but you could just leave it plain.

PARIS BREST

Serves 6–8

1 quantity choux pastry (see page 20)

2 tbsp flaked almonds

For the mousseline filling

600g warm crème pâtissière
  (see page 28)

400g butter, softened

150ml double cream

225g hazelnut paste

For the topping

200g caster sugar

50g toasted flaked almonds

Make the choux pastry following the method on page 20.

Preheat the oven to 200°C/400°F/Gas mark 6 and line a baking sheet with silicone paper. Draw a 30cm circle onto the paper then flip the paper over and place on the tray.

Spoon the choux pastry into a piping bag fitted with a 1cm plain nozzle and pipe, using swirls or lines, into one large ring, using the line as a template. If you like, you can draw an inner circle as a guide. Scatter the flaked almonds over the top of the choux.

Place a heatproof container of water into the oven on the base or bottom shelf to create steam. Bake the choux ring for 20 minutes. Open the oven door, remove the water container then shut the door, drop the oven temperature to 180°C/350°F/Gas mark 4 and continue to bake for another 20 minutes until golden brown and crisp. The water helps with the steam to start with, but you need to remove it to get a nice crusty result. Remove the choux ring from the tray and cool on a wire rack.

To make the mousseline filling, prepare the crème pâtissière. Beat half the butter into the warm crème pâtissière then allow to cool to room temperature. Beat in the rest of the butter, the cream and the hazelnut paste – you will end up with a smooth, light filling. Spoon it into a piping bag fitted with a plain 1cm nozzle.

Split the choux ring in half horizontally using a sharp, serrated knife and turning the ring as you cut. Place the base on a serving plate. Pipe the mousseline filling over the base then top with other half of the ring.

Heat a frying pan until hot, then add the sugar and cook until the sugar becomes liquid and turns a deep golden caramel colour. Add the toasted flaked almonds and stir through, then drizzle straight over the top of the filled choux. Allow to cool for a few minutes so that it hardens slightly before serving.

The inspiration for this came from quince tarte Tatins
we served alongside a partridge dish at the restaurant.
I loved the idea of quinces cooked in a tarte Tatin, so
we turned the quince trimmings into a purée, then
added a nice quince sorbet and a white chocolate snow
(you should be able to get maltodextrin from specialist
suppliers – see page 188). The combination of these three
elements works so well on the plate that I think this is
one of the best-looking desserts out there.

QUINCE TATIN WITH PURÉED QUINCE, QUINCE SORBET AND WHITE CHOCOLATE SNOW

Serves 6

350g puff pastry (see page 12), or good-
quality, bought all-butter puff pastry

flour, for dusting

Quince Sorbet (see page 45), to serve

1 tbsp celery cress

For the quince

75g sugar

25g butter

400ml water

juice of ½ lemon

3 large quince (about 500–600g) peeled,
cored and quartered

For the caramel

120g caster sugar

For the chocolate snow

50g white chocolate

50g maltodextrin

First of all, prepare the quince. Put the sugar,
butter, water and lemon juice in a saucepan
and bring to a simmer. Add the quince and
simmer for 30 minutes until tender. Lift the
quince out and cut the cheeks from them,
then stamp out six 6cm rounds from these,
using a cutter. Place on a plate lined with
kitchen paper.

Put three-quarters of the remaining quince
pieces in a blender with 50ml of the cooking
liquid. Blitz these to a purée, adding more
liquid if necessary, then spoon into a squeezy
bottle and set aside. Set the last few pieces
aside to use when serving.

Preheat the oven to 180°C/350°F/Gas mark 4.
Butter a 6-hole Yorkshire pudding tin, or
shallow muffin tin. To make the caramel,
put the caster sugar in a frying pan and heat
gently, without stirring, until the sugar turns
golden brown and liquid. Remove from the
heat, divide amongst the holes in the tin and
set aside to cool slightly. Place the discs of
quince, rounded side down, into the caramel.

Roll out the pastry on a lightly floured surface
to a thickness of 5mm, then cut out 6 circles,
each 1cm bigger than the holes in your tin.
Cover the quince with the pastry discs,
tucking the excess pastry in around the edges.
Bake in the oven for 15–20 minutes until the
pastry is golden brown and cooked through.

While the Tatins cook, make the chocolate
snow. Melt the chocolate in a heatproof
bowl set over a pan of simmering water.
The bowl should not touch the water.
Remove from the heat, add the maltodextrin
powder and beat until it forms breadcrumbs.

Remove the Tatins from the oven and leave
to rest for 1 minute before turning out: place
a flat baking tray over the top of the tin,
then tip the tin over so the Tatins all come
out together.

Place a Tatin on each plate and dress the plate
with a few swirls of quince purée. Place a ball
of Quince Sorbet alongside and finish with a
pile of chocolate snow and some celery cress.

This lovely tart uses Bramley apple purée for a hint of sharpness, which balances the butter and sugar glaze beautifully. I like to leave the skin on the sliced apples, so they hold together whilst they are cooking. When the apple tart comes out of the oven, just brush it with a little bit of melted butter, then serve with a scoop of vanilla ice cream for a simple dessert.

ROASTED APPLE TART

Serves 4–6

300g pâte sablée (see page 17)

flour, for dusting

250g Bramley apples, peeled, cored and roughly chopped

75g butter

25g caster sugar, plus extra for sprinkling

2–3 Cox's apples, unpeeled and finely sliced on a mandolin

Preheat the oven to 190°C/375°F/Gas mark 5 and line a baking sheet with silicone paper.

Roll out the pastry on a lightly floured surface to a 25cm x 18cm rectangle, about 5mm thick. Using a knife, score a border 1cm in from the edge, all the way around the rectangle, taking care not to cut all the way through the pastry. Transfer to the baking sheet and chill in the fridge while you make the filling.

Put the Bramley apples into a saucepan with 25g of the butter, 1 tablespoon water and the caster sugar. Cover and cook over a medium heat for 5 minutes, then stir and cover once more. Cook for another 5 minutes until the apple has cooked through, then stir them until they break down into a loose purée. Check the sweetness and add some more sugar if necessary, then set aside to cool.

When the apple is cool, remove the pastry from the fridge and spread the purée all over the base, keeping within the border. Layer the sliced Cox's apples all over the top, making lines up and down the length of the rectangle and overlapping them slightly. Melt the remaining butter and brush over the top of the apples, then sprinkle with the last of the caster sugar. Bake in the oven for about 18–20 minutes until the pastry is cooked through and the apples are lightly caramelised.

When the tart comes out of the oven, lightly char the edges of the apples with a blow torch or place under a hot grill then brush with any remaining melted butter. Serve hot, warm or cold.

Frangipane really is one of the easiest tart fillings to make – just use really good-quality almonds to give you depth of flavour, and remember to add the eggs gradually. A dash of apricot brandy doesn't hurt, either! For a light-textured frangipane, mix it really well – but make sure you don't overfill the tart with this airy mixture, as the filling will expand in the oven and you don't want it to explode out of the tart case as it cooks.

ROASTED APRICOT FRANGIPANE TART

Serves 12–16

1 quantity pâte sucrée (see page 16)

flour, for dusting

75g apricot jam

2 x 400g tins apricot halves in fruit juice, drained

100g butter, softened

100g caster sugar

2 eggs

1 egg yolk

50g self-raising flour

125g ground almonds

50ml stock syrup glaze (see page 29)

Roll out the pastry on a lightly floured surface to a thickness of 3mm. Carefully line a 23cm deep-sided, loose-bottomed tart tin with the pastry, pressing the pastry into the edges of the tin.

Spread the apricot jam over the base, then leave to rest in the fridge while you prepare the filling.

Preheat the oven to 190°C/375°F/Gas mark 5.

For the filling, beat the butter and sugar together in a bowl until pale and fluffy. Add the eggs and egg yolk, one at a time, beating well after each addition, until they have all been fully incorporated into the mixture. Fold in the flour and ground almonds carefully.

Spoon the frangipane filling into a piping bag and pipe into the base of the tart case in concentric circles.

Place the apricot halves upright into the mixture around the outer edge of the filling, stone side facing forwards, so they form a ring around the tart. Repeat with a second ring inside the first, then a final one in the middle – they should be lined up like dominos! Bake in the oven for 60–75 minutes until the filling is golden brown, puffed up slightly between the apricots and darker brown around the edges.

When the tart comes out of the oven, brush the apricots with the stock syrup glaze. Serve hot, warm or cold with crème fraîche or double cream.

I love making this – not least because I get a bumper harvest of plums from my garden every year, and I need to use them up before the wasps get to them. They're great for chutneys, of course, but this plum tart is brilliant. If you have puff pastry in the freezer, just defrost it and pin it out, then spread with crème pâtissière and lay the plums on top. Flash the tart in a nice hot oven, and you have the perfect dessert for summer and early autumn.

ROASTED PLUM TART WITH CRÈME PÂTISSIÈRE

Serves 8–10

butter, for greasing

flour, for dusting

500g puff pastry (see page 12), or good-quality, bought all-butter puff pastry

100g crème pâtissière (see page 28)

8 plums, halved, stoned and cut into wedges

50g melted butter

Preheat the oven to 220°C/450°F/Gas mark 7. Grease a large baking sheet and line with silicone paper.

Roll out the pastry on a lightly floured surface to a rectangle 15cm x 30cm and 5mm thick. Transfer to the lined baking sheet.

Score a border about 1cm in, all the way around the rectangle, taking care not to cut all the way through, then spread the inside with the crème pâtissière. Lay the plums, cut side up, in rows all over the crème pâtissière until it is covered.

Bake in the oven for 25 minutes until the pastry is cooked through and the plums are tender and caramelised, then brush with the melted butter.

Serve hot, warm or at room temperature, with vanilla ice cream or custard, if you like.

This delicious variation on treacle tart was inspired by a plain sugar tart I had whilst filming in the US and staying in an Amish community. Called shoo-fly pie because of the need to chase away the flies lured by its sticky sweetness, it was made mainly with molasses sugar, which gave it a deep, dark flavour.

MUSCOVADO SUGAR TART

Serves 10–12

butter, for greasing

1 quantity pâte brisée (see page 14)

flour, for dusting

1 egg yolk, for blind-baking

200g dark muscovado sugar

200g golden syrup

2 eggs

zest and juice of 1 lemon

1 tsp fine sea salt

125g fresh breadcrumbs

Preheat the oven to 180°C/350°F/Gas mark 4. Grease a 26cm diameter and 3cm deep loose-bottomed tart tin.

Roll out the pastry on a lightly floured surface to a thickness of 3mm and line the tart tin, then blind bake (see page 18). Remove from the oven and lower the temperature to 150°C/300°F/Gas mark 2.

Beat the sugar, golden syrup, eggs, lemon zest and juice and salt together in a bowl then fold in the breadcrumbs. Pour into the blind-baked tart case and smooth the top over. Bake in the oven for 50–60 minutes until golden and just spongy to the touch.

Remove and cool on a wire rack for 10 minutes before turning out. Serve hot or cold with whipped cream or vanilla ice cream.

Sea salt is a fantastic thing to add to caramel to cut its sweetness. You do need to proceed with caution, as salt can easily overpower other ingredients, but the combination of candied walnuts and sea salt in this caramel tart is a classic match that works every time.

WALNUT AND SEA SALT CARAMEL TARTS

Makes 4

butter, for greasing

1 quantity pâte sucrée (see page 16)

flour, for dusting

1 egg yolk, for blind-baking

100g caster sugar

100g walnut halves, roughly chopped

400g tin caramel

2 pinches of sea salt

Preheat the oven to 200°C/400°F/Gas mark 6. Grease four 8cm loose-bottomed tart tins and line a baking sheet with silicone paper.

Roll out the pastry on a lightly floured surface to a thickness of 3mm and use to line the tins, then blind bake (see page 18). Remove from the oven and leave to cool. Turn the oven down to 180°C/350°F/Gas mark 4.

Heat the sugar in a pan until golden brown and liquid all the way through – do not stir. Add the chopped walnuts and stir through, then pour onto the lined baking sheet and leave for a few minutes until set.

When the nuts are cool enough to touch, roughly chop them, then tip into a bowl and mix with the caramel and a pinch of salt. Spoon the mixture into the blind-baked tart cases and return to the oven for 10 minutes.

Serve the tarts warm or at room temperature with an extra pinch of sea salt, accompanied by clotted cream, vanilla ice cream or crème fraîche.

The idea for this came from a friend of mine, who also happens to be one of the greatest chefs in the world, Pierre Koffmann. Whenever I go to The Berkeley, I always have the rum babas. With plenty of rum in the syrup, and a dollop of cream, this is a French brasserie classic that should be served in all restaurants. Mr Koffmann serves it in his – and, let's face it, as one of very few chefs to have been at the helm of three consecutive, three-Michelin-starred restaurants, he must know a thing or two.

RUM BABAS

Makes 8

50g caster sugar

15g fresh yeast

75ml warm milk

2 eggs, beaten

75g butter, softened, plus extra
  for greasing

300g strong flour

For the syrup

200g light brown soft sugar

200ml water

100ml dark rum

To serve

200ml double cream

1 tsp vanilla bean paste

Put the sugar, yeast and warm milk into a large bowl and whisk together until the yeast has dissolved. Add the eggs and butter and beat to combine. Add the flour and continue mixing until the batter is very smooth and comes away from the side of the bowl.

Grease 8 individual 6cm baba moulds and divide the mixture between them, filling each one approximately half full. Set aside to rest in a warm place for 20–30 minutes, or until the mixture has doubled in size. Meanwhile, preheat the oven to 200°C/400°F/Gas mark 6.

Place the moulds on a baking tray and bake for 10–15 minutes, or until golden, then remove from the oven and leave to cool in the moulds. When cool, remove from the moulds and set aside.

For the syrup, put the sugar and 200ml water into a pan and bring to the boil. Boil for 2 minutes, then remove from the heat and add the rum. Place the babas in the rum syrup to soak, two at a time.

Lightly whip the cream and vanilla bean paste to soft peaks. Serve the soaked rum babas with the whipped cream.

CHOCOLATE CAKES

As its name suggests, this cake is from Smith Island, a small island in America's Chesapeake Bay. The story goes that the fishermen's wives would make this multi-layered cake for their menfolk to take with them on their long sea voyages, as the chocolate icing kept the cake moist. It takes a bit of time to get the layers looking sharp, but all you need is concentration and patience.

SMITH ISLAND CAKE

Serves 6–8

50g butter, melted, plus extra for greasing

6 eggs

175g caster sugar

100g plain flour

75g cocoa powder, sifted

100g white chocolate (optional)

mixed berries, to decorate

For the chestnut filling

300g chestnut purée

100ml double cream

For the icing

250g dark chocolate (70% cocoa solids), finely chopped

50g cocoa powder, sifted

100g icing sugar, sifted

25ml water

Preheat the oven to 200°C/400°F/Gas mark 6 and grease and line a 22cm cake tin.

Whisk the eggs and sugar together until the mixture has doubled in volume and leaves a trail from the whisk. Fold in the flour and cocoa powder. Pour into the tin and bake for 30–35 minutes.

Remove from the oven and leave to cool in the tin for 10 minutes. Turn the cake out onto a wire rack and leave to cool.

To make the filling, whisk the chestnut purée and double cream together.

To make the icing, place the chopped chocolate, the cocoa powder, icing sugar and water in a saucepan and set over a low heat. Heat until the mixture is liquid, then whisk together until smooth.

To assemble the cake, slice it into horizontal layers, using a long, serrated knife. Sandwich the layers together with the chestnut cream.

Place on a cake stand and pour the chocolate icing over the whole cake, making sure it covers the top and sides.

If you want to write on the cake, melt the white chocolate in a heatproof bowl over a pan of simmering water. The base of the bowl should not touch the water. Spoon the melted chocolate into a piping bag and pipe the words, 'Smith Island' on the top, if you like. Decorate with berries.

The secret to this cake is to use good-quality cocoa and nice strong espresso. With weaker coffee, the temptation is to keep adding more to get the right depth of coffee flavour, but this will unbalance the recipe.

CHOCOLATE AND ESPRESSO CAKE

Serves 12–16

50ml strong espresso coffee

75ml hot water

90g cocoa powder

275g butter, softened, plus extra for greasing

375ml sour cream

275g dark brown soft sugar

4 eggs

1 tbsp vanilla bean paste

300g plain flour

2 tsp baking powder

1 tsp bicarbonate of soda

½ tsp fine sea salt

Preheat the oven to 180C°/350°F/Gas mark 4 and grease and line a 23cm deep-sided, loose-bottomed cake tin.

Place the coffee and hot water in bowl then sift the cocoa over the top and whisk together to form a smooth paste. Stir in the sour cream and whisk once more.

Beat the butter and sugar together in a food mixer, or in a bowl with an electric whisk, for at least 5 minutes until lightened and fluffy. Add the eggs, one at a time, beating between each addition. Beat in the vanilla paste and sour-cream mixture – the mixture will curdle slightly but do not worry. Sift the flour, baking powder, bicarbonate of soda and salt into the mixture, then fold in to combine.

Pour into the prepared cake tin and bake for 45-60 minutes until risen and slightly firm to the touch. A skewer inserted into the centre of the cake should come out clean – if it doesn't, return the cake to the oven for a further 5 minutes.

Remove from the oven and cool in the tin before turning out. Serve on its own or with a dollop of clotted cream.

The impressive marbling in this cake is surprisingly easy to achieve: all it needs is some subtle swirling with a spoon. It doesn't get much more low-tech than that!

MARBLED CHOCOLATE CAKE

Serves 8–10

360g butter, softened, plus extra
   for greasing

420g icing sugar

7 eggs

50ml milk

420g plain flour

3 tsp baking powder

100g dark chocolate (70% cocoa solids),
   roughly chopped

Preheat the oven to 170°C/325°F/Gas mark 3 and grease and line the base of a 1kg loaf tin.

Put the butter into a kitchen mixer or large bowl, sift in the icing sugar and beat until fluffy. Add the eggs, one by one, beating between each addition. Fold in the milk, flour and baking powder and mix gently to combine, then take half the mixture and place it in a clean bowl.

Melt the dark chocolate in a heatproof bowl over a pan of simmering water. The bowl should not touch the water. Remove and cool slightly. Whisk the melted dark chocolate into one half of the cake mixture until it is fully incorporated.

Place the chocolate batter into the bottom of the tin and spread it out to cover the base. Spread the plain mixture over the top. Gently run a spoon through the mixture, lifting the chocolate up over the plain mixture a couple of times through the length of the tin.

Bake in the oven for 60 minutes until light golden brown and risen. A skewer inserted into the centre of the cake should come out clean – if it doesn't, return the cake to the oven for a further 5 minutes and repeat.

Cool in the tin completely before turning out onto a wire rack and serving.

The deep, dark flavour of stout adds another dimension to this chocolate cake sandwiched with a fluffy cream cheese frosting. Not only does the stout add flavour, but colour and texture too.

STOUT AND DARK CHOCOLATE CAKE
WITH CREAM CHEESE FROSTING

Serves 8–10

250ml stout

100g cocoa powder

1 tsp bicarbonate of soda

350g soft light brown sugar

4 eggs

180ml crème fraîche

250g self-raising flour

1 pinch salt

For the frosting

100g cream cheese

50g icing sugar

45ml double cream

To serve (optional)

peanut butter

Nutella (chocolate and hazelnut spread)

baby marshmallows, toasted

praline, crumbled

edible flowers, such as pansies

Preheat the oven to 170°C/325°F/Gas mark 3. Grease and line a 23cm springform cake tin.

Pour the stout into a saucepan and bring to a simmer, then add the cocoa powder and bicarbonate of soda and whisk until smooth. Remove from the heat.

Whisk the sugar and eggs together in a bowl until just combined. Add the crème fraîche, then the warm stout mixture and whisk together. Sift in the flour and salt. Fold together, then pour into the prepared cake tin and bake for 40 minutes until risen and firm to the touch.

Leave to cool in the tin for 10 minutes, then turn out and cool on a wire rack.

Meanwhile, place the cream cheese in a bowl and sift in the icing sugar. Beat together until softened and fluffy. In a separate bowl, whip the double cream to soft peaks, then fold it into the cream-cheese mixture. Split the cake in half horizontally and spread the frosting over the bottom half of the cake, then place the other half on top.

Serve the cake as it is, or slice it into thirds and place on a large serving plate over discs of peanut butter and Nutella, made with a circular template cut from a piece of card. Scatter a row of toasted baby marshmallows and crumbled praline alongside, and top with some edible pansies.

This speciality from Bordeaux is traditionally made in copper moulds. Of course, you can now get fancy silicone versions, but they don't give you quite the same crunchy finish. These cakes are generally flavoured with rum and vanilla, but I've added cocoa to the batter and put cherries in the middle for an extra treat.

CHOCOLATE AND CHERRY CANNELÉS

Makes 8

250ml milk

25g butter, plus extra for greasing

1 tsp vanilla bean paste

100g caster sugar

1 egg

1 egg yolk

25g plain flour

25g cocoa powder

16 maraschino cherries, halved

Preheat the oven to 240°C/475°F/Gas mark 9 and butter 8 cannelé moulds really well, or grease lightly if using silicone moulds.

Place the milk, butter and the vanilla bean paste into a saucepan and heat until just simmering. Meanwhile, whisk the sugar, egg and egg yolk together in a large bowl and sift the flour and cocoa powder onto the mixture, then whisk together. Pour the hot milk onto the egg mixture and whisk together until it forms a thick batter.

Pour into the moulds until they are three-quarters full, then drop a few pieces of cherry into the centre of each mould. Place on a baking tray and cook in the oven for 10 minutes, then lower the oven temperature to 190°C/375°F/Gas mark 5 and cook for another 30–35 minutes until dark brown and slightly domed.

Remove from the moulds straight away and turn out onto a wire rack to cool. They need to develop a firm crust, so it's best to turn them out as quickly as possible so they don't steam in the moulds and soften.

Here the marbling is achieved by sandwiching the two different doughs with the Nutella and banana, then giving the dough a couple of judicious twists before laying it in the tin. The yeasted dough rises in the oven to create a distinctive marbling. Eat this cake either hot out of the oven or at room temperature, so it's not too heavy.

BANANA AND NUTELLA MARBLED CAKE

Serves 6–8

1 quantity enriched yeast dough (see page 24), plus 15g cocoa powder

150g Nutella (chocolate hazelnut spread)

2 bananas, peeled and cut into 1cm slices

100ml stock syrup glaze (see page 29)

Make up the dough following the recipe on page 24, up to the proving stage. Divide the dough in half and place one half in a bowl. Mix the cocoa powder with 1–2 tsp water and add this to the other half of the dough. Knead until totally combined, then place in a separate bowl. Cover both bowls of dough loosely. Leave them to prove for 4 hours at room temperature. Alternatively, cover and leave in the fridge overnight.

Grease and line the base of a 23cm springform tin.

Knock the chocolate dough back and pin it out (pull it out slightly, then roll it) to a rectangle about 15cm x 50cm. Spread the Nutella over the top of the dough, right to the edges, then place the banana slices all over the dough.

Pin out the plain dough to a rectangle the same size, and lay this over the top of the banana-topped dough. Press down lightly, then cut in half lengthways. Holding either end of one piece, twist in opposite directions and lay carefully into the cake tin. Twist the other half in the same way and fold into the centre of the first half.

Leave to prove for 2 hours, covered, in a warm place until doubled in size. Preheat the oven to 180°C/350°F/Gas mark 4.

Bake for 35–40 minutes until golden brown and risen. The base should sound hollow when tapped. Brush with the stock syrup glaze then leave to cool on a wire rack.

CAKES WITH FRUIT

With a cake this simple, success depends on the quality of your ingredients. Just like balsamic vinegar, maple syrup is graded – and, as with the premium grades of balsamic, you get what you pay for.

BLUEBERRY AND MAPLE SYRUP BAKE

Makes 12–16

1 quantity pâte sûcrée (see page 16)

200g blueberry jam

225g butter, softened, plus extra
 for greasing

200g light muscovado sugar

275g self-raising flour, plus extra
 for dusting

2 tsp baking powder

1 tsp ground cinnamon

4 large eggs

200ml maple syrup

150g blueberries

3 tbsp demerara sugar

Preheat the oven to 180°C/350°F/Gas mark 4 and grease and line the base of a 30cm x 23cm, straight-sided frame or traybake tin.

Roll out the pâte sûcrée on a lightly floured surface to 5mm thick and 1cm larger than the frame or tin. Place on a silicone-lined tray then cover with another sheet of silicone paper and a tray the same size. Place in the oven for 15 minutes until golden and cooked through. Trim to the same size as the frame or tin then place inside. Cover with the blueberry jam then set aside.

Place the butter, sugar, flour, baking powder, cinnamon, eggs and 100ml of the maple syrup in a food mixer or large bowl and beat for a couple of minutes until a smooth batter is formed. Pour into the prepared tin and smooth out to the edges. Scatter the blueberries over the batter, then finish by sprinkling over the demerera sugar.

Bake in the oven for 35–40 minutes, until golden brown and risen. A skewer inserted into the centre of the cake should come out clean – if it doesn't, return the cake to the oven for a further 5 minutes and repeat.

Pour the remaining maple syrup over the top, before leaving the cake to cool in the tin. Cut into rectangles to serve.

This looks elaborate, but in actual fact it is surprisingly simple to make, as long as you have the right mould for baking the brioche. In keeping with the Christmas theme, I've decorated the garland with a layer of royal icing 'snow' and some really beautiful glacé fruit. (If you want to have a go at making your own, there's a recipe in my previous desserts book.)

CANDIED FRUIT CHRISTMAS GARLAND

Serves 8–10

1 quantity brioche dough (see page 22)

butter, for greasing

50ml spiced rum

zest of 1 orange

zest of 1 lemon

300g candied fruit, such as pears, tangerines, cherries and angelica, roughly chopped

50g sultanas

flour, for dusting

100ml stock syrup glaze (see page 29)

200g royal icing (see page 41)

150g whole glacé fruit, halved or sliced

Make the brioche dough and prove it for 1½ hours (instead of the 2 hours in step 4 of the brioche dough recipe).

Generously butter a 24cm bundt tin or savarin mould. Place the rum, orange and lemon zest, candied fruit and sultanas in a bowl and leave to soak for 20 minutes. Take about 60g of the fruit and scatter into the buttered tin.

Lightly flour a work surface then tip the dough out onto it and gently knock the air out of the dough. Spread it out to a large rectangle about 50cm x 30cm and scatter the remaining soaked fruit over the dough. Roll into a large sausage shape about 50cm long, then twist round into a circle, joining the ends together. Transfer to the prepared tin, cover and leave to rise for 1½ hours in a warm place.

Preheat the oven to 190°C/375°F/Gas mark 5.

Bake for 30 minutes until golden brown and hollow when tapped on the base of the ring. Remove, turn out upside down and brush with the stock syrup glaze, then leave to cool on a wire rack.

When cold, spread the royal icing on the top and decorate with the glacé fruit.

It was in France that my love of pastry-work and dessert-making began. If I'm honest, it was by chance, as the pastry chef went off to the loo and nobody ever saw him again! So, within 48 hours, I was promoted. It was an incredible learning curve, and one I have no regrets about. France is synonymous with wonderful pastry-work, desserts and cakes, and this simple lemon cake is just one of the many classic French recipes you'll find in this book.

CLASSIC FRENCH LEMON CAKE

Serves 8–10

For the cake

75g butter, plus extra for greasing

3 eggs

juice and zest of 2 lemons

200g caster sugar

75g crème fraîche

150g plain or cake flour (a very fine plain flour, such as 00)

1 tsp baking powder

For the glaze

75g icing sugar

juice of 1 lemon

Preheat the oven to 170°C/325°F/Gas mark 3 and grease and line the base of a 1kg loaf tin.

Melt the butter then allow it to cool slightly. Place the eggs, lemon juice and sugar in a food mixer or large bowl and whisk for a few minutes until totally combined and the sugar has dissolved.

Whisk the cooled butter and crème fraîche into the egg-and-lemon mixture, then sift the flour and baking powder over the top and gently fold in. Stir in the lemon zest and spoon into the prepared loaf tin.

Place in the oven and bake for 45–60 minutes until golden and risen – the cake should split along its top. A skewer inserted into the centre of the cake should come out clean – if it doesn't, return the cake to the oven for a further 5 minutes and repeat.

Remove from the oven and allow to cool for 10 minutes on a wire rack, then turn out and place back on the rack, over a shallow tray.

Whisk the icing sugar and lemon juice together in a bowl then pour the icing over the warm cake.

Remove the tray from underneath the rack and pour any excess icing from the tray back into the bowl. Return the tray to sit under the rack and spoon the glaze over the cake once again. Leave on the rack to cool completely before serving.

This is a firm favourite with my chefs – I hope you like it as much as they do! Sifting the flour and sugar several times before adding them to the batter helps to create the ethereally light texture that gives this cake its name.

ANGEL FOOD SAVARIN CAKE
WITH RASPBERRY CÔMPOTE

Serves 8–10

For the cake
butter, for greasing
125g plain flour
200g caster sugar
9 large egg whites
2 tsp vanilla extract
1 tsp cream of tartar
½ tsp salt
For the compote
185g icing sugar
350g raspberries

Preheat the oven to 180°C/350°F/Gas mark 4. Grease only the base of a 25cm angel food cake tin.

Sieve the flour and 175g of the caster sugar into a bowl, then repeat twice more – the flour and sugar need to have plenty of air.

Whisk the egg whites, vanilla extract, cream of tartar and salt together in a food mixer or large bowl with an electric whisk, until soft peaks start to form. Make sure the bowl and whisk are very clean, free of grease and completely dry, as any grease or water will affect the meringue.

Add the remaining caster sugar and whisk until shiny, glossy and still slightly soft – you don't want it to get to the stiff-peaks stage.

Sprinkle a quarter of the flour-and-sugar mixture over the top then fold in quickly, trying to keep as much air in the mixture as possible. Repeat with the remaining flour and sugar in three more batches until it is all incorporated.

Spoon into the tin, taking care to be gentle with the mixture, then tap once to release any air pockets. Place in the oven and bake for 30 minutes until golden brown and slightly firm when pressed.

Place upside down over a wire rack until completely cold. Then, turn the tin upright, use a knife to loosen the sides of the cake and turn it out onto a plate.

Sieve 160g of the icing sugar into a bowl and mix it with 1–2 tbsp water to form a runny icing. Drizzle this all over the cake and let it set slightly.

Place 200g of the raspberries into a blender or processor and blitz to a purée with the remaining icing sugar. Pass through a fine sieve, then stir in the rest of the raspberries. Spoon over the top of the cake, or slice the cake and serve alongside.

Yuzu has become increasingly popular over recent years, to the point where you can now find yuzu juice in some supermarkets. With a taste somewhere between mandarin and lime, the juice of this Japanese citrus fruit makes a great contrast to the richness of chocolate, but here it magically accentuates the flavour of a simple apple cake.

APPLE CAKE WITH YUZU CARAMEL

Serves 6–8

For the cake

butter, for greasing

6 eggs

300g light brown soft sugar

250g plain flour

2 tsp baking powder

2 dessert apples, peeled and finely grated

For the apple filling

50g caster sugar

2 large Bramley apples, peeled, cored and roughly chopped

25g butter

4 tbsp water

For the caramel

100g light brown soft sugar

100g butter

200g double cream

1 tbsp yuzu juice

To serve

300ml double cream

1 tbsp yuzu juice

Preheat the oven to 180°C/350°F/Gas mark 4. Grease and line the base of a 23cm square tin.

Whisk the eggs and sugar in a food mixer, or in a bowl with an electric whisk, until thickened and very light in colour. Fold the flour and baking powder into the mixture, then quickly fold in the grated apples.

Spoon the batter into the prepared tin and bake in the oven for 25 minutes until risen and light golden brown. A skewer inserted into the centre of the cake should come out clean – if it doesn't, return to the oven for a further 5 minutes and repeat.

While the cake bakes, make the filling. Place the caster sugar in a saucepan and heat gently, without stirring, until it turns golden brown and liquid. Add the apples, butter and water and stir to combine. Cover and cook for 3–5 minutes until softened and just tender, but still chunky. Remove from the heat and set aside to cool.

While the filling cools, make the caramel. Place the sugar in a sauté pan and heat, without stirring, until melted and dark brown. Whisk in the butter, then add the cream and cook for 3–5 minutes until thickened. Stir in the yuzu juice then set aside to cool.

Whip the double cream to soft peaks, then stir in the yuzu juice and whisk again, to semi-firm peaks.

When the cake is cold, split it in half horizontally, using a sharp, serrated knife and turning the cake as you go. Spread the caramelised apple over the bottom half. Drizzle the caramel over the top then place the top half of the cake over this, pressing down lightly. Slice and serve with a spoonful of the yuzu cream.

I love this classic fruit and nut cake, which is an adaptation of a family recipe. I've always liked glacé fruit, but you do need to buy the good-quality sort. My favourite way to eat a slice of this is spread with just a little bit of unsalted butter.

GLACÉ FRUIT AND NUT CAKE

Serves 8–10

For the cake

225g butter, plus extra for greasing

225g caster sugar

1 vanilla pod, split and seeds scraped

4 large eggs

100g ground almonds

275g self-raising flour

125g sultanas

125g glacé cherries

125g raisins

For the decoration

150ml stock syrup glaze (see page 29)

50g whole, peeled almonds

75g red glacé cherries, halved

Preheat the oven to 150°C/300°F/Gas mark 2 and grease and line the base and sides of a 20cm round, deep-sided cake tin. Cover the outside of the tin with a layer of silicone paper and secure in place with kitchen string.

Beat the butter, sugar and vanilla seeds in a kitchen mixer or large bowl with an electric whisk, until really light and fluffy. Beat the eggs in, one at a time, then fold in the ground almonds and 200g of the flour. Place all the dried fruit in a bowl and toss with the rest of the flour so that they are all coated, then stir into the cake mixture until well combined.

Spoon into the lined cake tin, smooth the top over then bake for 1¾ hours until golden brown and risen – cover the top with baking parchment or foil half-way through if the top is colouring too much. A skewer inserted into the centre of the cake should come out clean – if it doesn't, return the cake to the oven for a further 5 minutes and repeat.

While the cake cooks, place the stock syrup in a small saucepan and heat until just simmering. Add the almonds and simmer for 3 minutes then lift out onto silicone paper. Drop the cherries into the syrup just to warm through then lift out and place them alongside the almonds.

When the cake is ready, remove and cool in the tin for 5 minutes then arrange the almonds and cherries in rings onto the top of the cake – they will stick to the surface. Leave to cool completely before removing from the tin and discarding the paper. Serve in wedges.

This is the kind of cake I like to make at home: it's really simple, but the crumble adds a nice crunchy texture. When peaches aren't in season, you can use tinned peaches – just drain them well before adding them to the cake batter. Plums and damsons also work well, but avoid fruit with a high water content, such as strawberries and raspberries, or you'll end up with a soggy cake.

PEACH AND CRÈME FRAÎCHE CRUMBLE CAKE

Serves 12–16

For the cake

450g self-raising flour

2 tsp baking powder

200g butter, plus extra for greasing

350g demerara sugar

6 eggs

150g crème fraîche

25ml peach schnapps or peach juice

100ml peach purée

7 peaches, halved and stoned, or
  2 x 400g tins peach halves, drained

For the crumble

60g plain flour

½ tsp ground cinnamon

30g butter, diced

30g demerara sugar

For the topping

100g crème fraîche

100g cream cheese

50ml double cream

Preheat the oven to 150°C/300°F/Gas mark 1 and grease and line a 24cm high-sided, loose-bottomed cake tin.

To make the cake, place the flour, baking powder and butter in a bowl and rub together to form a breadcrumb-like texture. Stir in the sugar.

In a separate bowl, whisk the eggs, crème fraîche, peach schnapps or juice, and purée together, then pour onto the dry mixture and mix to a thick batter.

Pour half into the prepared tin and tap the tin gently to settle the batter. Place the peach halves, cut-side up, onto the batter in concentric circles, then top with the remaining batter, smoothing over the top.

Bake in the centre of the oven for 1¾ hours until golden and risen. A skewer inserted into the centre of the cake should come out clean – if it doesn't, return the cake to the oven for a further 5 minutes and repeat. Leave the cake in the tin to cool completely.

While the cake cools, make the crumble to go on top. Turn the oven up to 180°C/350°F/Gas mark 4. Place the flour, ground cinnamon and butter in a bowl and rub until the mix resembles fine breadcrumbs. Add the sugar and stir to combine. Spread out over a baking sheet and bake for 6–8 minutes until golden brown and crispy. Set aside to cool on the baking sheet.

For the topping, whisk the crème fraîche, cream cheese and double cream together then spread over the cake while it's still in the tin – this will give you a neat finish. Scatter the crumble over the top to cover the cream then ease the cake out from the tin.

These simple-to-make and light-textured cakes are great for afternoon tea, or as a simple dessert. You can make them with other fruit too – try peaches or nectarines.

MERINGUE-TOPPED STRAWBERRY CAKES

Makes 12

For the cakes

70g roasted, chopped hazelnuts

135g butter, softened, plus extra
 for greasing

1 vanilla pod, split and seeds scraped

115g caster sugar

2 large eggs

115g plain flour

1 tsp baking powder

65ml double cream

For the topping

300g strawberries, hulled and
 roughly chopped

1 quantity Swiss meringue (see page 32)

To serve

strawberries and finely crumbled
 meringue (optional)

Preheat the oven to 180°C/350°F/Gas mark 4 and grease a 12-cup, loose-bottomed mini sandwich tin, with straight sides.

Whizz the chopped hazelnuts to a powder in a blender. Beat the butter, vanilla seeds and sugar together in a kitchen mixer, or in a bowl with an electric whisk, until light and fluffy. Beat the eggs in one at a time, then fold in the flour, baking powder and ground hazelnuts. Gently fold in the double cream then spoon into the sandwich tin and top with the chopped strawberries.

Place in the oven and bake for 20 minutes until the cakes are cooked through. Leave to cool in the tin for 5 minutes before turning them out.

Spoon the Swiss meringue into a piping bag and cut the tip off. Pipe the meringue on top of the strawberries in little peaks, or any other pattern you like. Glaze with a blow torch or under a hot grill until just golden. Serve warm or cold, with a line of strawberries and finely crumbled meringue, if liked.

This is a wonderful dish of contrasting flavours and textures, with crunch from the poppy seeds, sharpness from the lemon curd, saltiness from the olives, and the cooling sweetness of raspberry sorbet.

LEMON CURD AND POPPY SEED SPONGE
WITH GREEN OLIVE PURÉE AND RASPBERRY SORBET

Serves 12

For the lemon curd and poppy seed sponge

170g butter, softened

170g caster sugar

200g self-raising flour

½ tsp baking powder

3 eggs

1 tbsp poppy seeds

125g lemon curd

For the green olive purée

100g caster sugar

100ml water

100g pitted green olives

1 quantity Raspberry Sorbet (see page 45)

Preheat the oven to 170°C/325°F/Gas mark 3. Grease a 12-hole traybake tin or silicone mould.

Place the butter, sugar, flour, baking powder, eggs and poppy seeds in a food mixer or large bowl and beat for a couple of minutes until a smooth batter is formed. Fold the lemon curd into the mixture, taking care not to mix it in too much: you want to create a marbled effect throughout.

Spoon the mixture into the moulds, to about two-thirds full, then bake for 18–20 minutes until golden and risen. A skewer inserted into the centre of the cakes should come out clean – if it doesn't, return them to the oven for a further 5 minutes and repeat. Leave to cool in the tin for 5 minutes before turning out the cakes onto a wire rack.

Meanwhile, make the olive purée. Put the sugar, water and olives in a saucepan and bring to the boil. Simmer for 5 minutes, then pour into a food blender and blitz to a fine purée, taking care to leave the lid open a crack to release the steam.

Place the poppy seed sponge onto the plate, brush the olive purée alongside, and then finish with a spoonful of Raspberry Sorbet.

Peaches are perfect for this dessert, as the natural sugars in their juice cause the base of the cakes (which becomes the top, when served) to caramelise nicely. This recipe came from a peach farm I visited in the States a few years back. Each day, they made hundreds of these, using fruit picked the very same day, and people would travel from far and wide in their massive SUVs to buy them.

INDIVIDUAL PEACH UPSIDE-DOWN CAKES

Serves 12

For the topping

60g melted butter, plus extra for greasing

60g demerara sugar

3 peaches, stoned and cut into wedges

For the cake

3 eggs

85g caster sugar

85g plain flour

25g melted butter

Preheat the oven to 180°C/350°F/Gas mark 4. Grease and line the bases of a 12-hole mini traybake tin.

Divide the melted butter between the moulds and sprinkle in the demerara sugar – you need about a teaspoon in each mould. Lay 3 slices of peach on top, arranging them in a fan.

Place the eggs and sugar in a food mixer or large bowl and whisk until very pale and thickened. Sift the flour over the mixture and fold in, then fold in the melted butter.

Spoon the mixture into the tin, dividing the mixture equally between the 12 holes, then bake in the oven for 15–18 minutes until golden brown and risen. A skewer inserted into the centre of the cakes should come out clean – if it doesn't, return the cake to the oven for a further 5 minutes and repeat.

Leave to cool in the tin for 5 minutes then place a large baking tray with a small lip over the top of tin, flip it over and carefully lift the tin away. The cakes should slide out. Serve warm with custard.

TEATIME

Traditional Breton sablés are, I suppose, the French equivalent of our shortbread. These crisp, buttery biscuits can be either sweet or savoury – try sprinkling them lightly with parmesan cheese before baking for a snack to serve with drinks. Personally, I love them as they are: their texture is really fine and sandy (the word 'sablé' means sand in French), and they just crumble in the mouth.

BRETON SABLÉS WITH CRÈME PÂTISSIÈRE AND RASPBERRIES

Makes 8

For the Breton sablés

3 egg yolks

125g icing sugar

1 tsp vanilla bean paste

150g butter, softened

200g plain flour, plus extra for dusting

1 tsp baking powder

For the topping

200ml crème pâtissière (see page 28)

475g raspberries

1–2 tbsp raspberry powder

baby basil leaves, to serve

Preheat the oven to 170°C/325°F/Gas mark 3 and grease two 4-hole Yorkshire pudding tins (each hole around 8cm in diameter).

Whisk the egg yolks, icing sugar and vanilla bean paste in a kitchen mixer, or in a bowl with an electric whisk, until almost white and very fluffy. Beat in the butter, a little at a time, until completely smooth, then sift in the flour and baking powder. Fold together to form a soft dough. Transfer to a work surface dusted with flour, then flatten to a disc about 3cm thick. Cover with clingfilm and chill in the fridge for 30 minutes to firm up.

Remove the dough and roll out to a thickness of about 7mm. Stamp out 8 discs using an 8cm cutter and lay one in each mould.

Bake for 12–15 minutes until golden brown and risen, then remove and transfer to a wire rack. Remove the sablés from the tin whilst they are still warm, so they don't stick.

While the sablés are baking, make the crème pâtissière, then spoon into a piping bag fitted with a 5mm plain nozzle. Pipe little, individual peaks on top of each cooled sablé – around 12–14 on each. Top each peak with a raspberry.

Decorate by placing a teaspoon onto the serving plate, dusting with raspberry powder then removing the spoon, leaving a stencilled spoon alongside the sablé. Top with some baby basil leaves.

Essentially, this is just a standard fruit cake; however, you can vary the flavourings to suit your taste. Orange or lemon zest makes a nice addition, but I've also tried it with passionfruit. The alternative touch is the Easter rabbit, which is made with a simple caramel shaped in a plasticine mould – make sure there are no air bubbles in the caramel prior to pouring it into the mould. Beyond that, it all comes down to practice and your piping skills...

ALTERNATIVE SIMNEL CAKE
WITH EASTER BUNNY

Serves 10–12

175g butter, softened, plus extra
  for greasing

175g dark brown soft sugar

3 eggs

50ml milk

175g self-raising flour

2 tsp mixed spice

1 tsp ground ginger

25g ground almonds

90g cherries, washed and dried,
  then quartered

90g stem ginger, finely chopped

90g sultanas

90g dried apricots, roughly chopped

90g dried cranberries

1kg natural marzipan

250g good-quality plasticine

olive oil, for brushing

200g caster sugar

green food colouring

100g royal icing (see page 41)

3 tbsp apricot jam, warmed

Preheat the oven 170C/325/Gas mark 3 and grease and line the base and sides of a 20cm deep, round cake tin. Beat the butter and sugar until fluffy and light. Beat the eggs in, one at a time, then fold in the milk, flour, spices, almonds, cherries, ginger and dried fruit. Spoon half the mixture into the prepared tin and level the surface.

On a surface dusted with icing sugar, roll the marzipan into a circle the same size as the tin. Place on top of the cake mixture, then spoon over the remaining mixture and level the surface. Bake for 1¾–2 hours or until golden brown, risen and firm in the middle (cover with baking parchment if the top is getting too dark). A skewer inserted into the centre should come out clean. Leave the cake to cool in the tin before turning out onto a rack.

Cut out a cardboard template of a 15cm-high rabbit and draw on any details you want. Draw and cut out a separate 12cm circle. Roll out some plasticine to 1cm thick and place the rabbit on top. Cut through the plasticine so you have a rabbit-shaped hole, then transfer to a silicone-lined mat on a flat tray, discarding

the inner rabbit. Brush the inside edges of the hole with oil. Repeat with the circle.

Heat the sugar in a pan until golden and liquid all through. Set the base of the pan in cold water to stop the caramel overheating, then pour into the rabbit mould to 3mm thick. Leave to set hard. Add a few drops of green colouring to the remaining caramel, and swirl to combine. Pour the green caramel into the circle mould to a depth of 3mm then leave to set hard. Spoon the icing into a small piping bag and decorate the rabbit, placing it over the original template and tracing any details. Roll the remaining marzipan out to 3mm then cut a disc out the same size as the cake. Brush the cake with warmed apricot jam then lay the marzipan on top. Roll the remaining marzipan into 13 balls and place around the edge of the cake. Place under a hot grill or glaze with a blow torch until just golden.

Set the green disc in the centre of the cake. Warm the base of the rabbit in a hot pan to melt the caramel slightly, then stick to the green disc. Press down gently, leaving the rabbit upright in the middle.

Almond and oil cake might be nothing new, but my version uses rapeseed oil. This fantastic ingredient is growing in popularity, and I like to use it instead of olive oil when I want a milder, more delicate flavour.

ALMOND AND RAPESEED OIL CAKE

Serves 6–8

4 eggs

200g caster sugar

75g melted butter, cooled

150ml extra-virgin rapeseed oil

100g polenta

1 tsp poppy seeds

1 tsp baking powder

200g ground almonds

45g toasted flaked almonds

50ml stock syrup glaze (see page 29)

Preheat the oven to 180°C/350°F/Gas mark 4. Grease and line a 20cm springform cake tin.

Whisk the eggs and sugar together in a food mixer, or in a bowl with an electric whisk, until very pale and fluffy. Pour in the cooled, melted butter and the rapeseed oil, continuing to whisk all the time.

Fold the polenta, poppy seeds, baking powder and ground almonds gently into the mixture until fully combined – it should be a thick batter.

Pour into the prepared tin then bake for 30–35 minutes until golden and risen. A skewer inserted into the centre should come out clean – if it doesn't, return the cake to the oven for a further 5 minutes and repeat.

Cool in the tin for 15 minutes before turning out, face down, onto a serving plate. Warm the stock syrup glaze in a small saucepan. Scatter the flaked almonds over the cake then drizzle over the stock syrup glaze. Serve with a little whipped cream, if you like.

Browning the butter really well before adding it to the batter gives this cake an extra dimension of flavour. Nut-brown butter is often used in savoury dishes for its complexity, but in sweet dishes it contributes quite an unusual taste. This cake is perfect for afternoon tea, or simply to have at home so everyone can help themselves to a slice.

BROWN BUTTER AND PLUM CAKE

Serves 6–8

For the cake

225g butter, plus extra for greasing

200g light brown soft sugar

4 eggs

1 tsp vanilla extract

200g self-raising flour, plus extra for dusting

For the filling

400g plums, halved, stoned and quartered

50g light brown soft sugar

½ tsp ground cinnamon

175ml double cream

1–2 tbsp icing sugar, for dusting

Preheat the oven to 190°C/375°F/Gas mark 5 and grease and flour two 20cm sandwich tins.

Heat the butter in a saucepan over a high heat for a couple of minutes, or place in a heatproof bowl, covered, in a microwave, until nut-brown. Pass through a fine sieve into the bowl of a kitchen mixer or large bowl and set aside to cool completely.

When it's nearly set firm, place 25g of the browned butter into a small pan and set aside. Add the sugar to the larger amount in the bowl and beat until fluffy, then add the eggs, one by one.

Add the vanilla extract then sift in the flour and fold in to combine. Pour the mixture into the prepared tins and bake for 20–25 minutes until golden and risen. A skewer inserted into the centre of the cake should come out clean – if it doesn't, return to the oven for a further 5 minutes and repeat.

While the cakes bake, make the plum filling. Add the plums to the small pan with the nut-brown butter. Add the sugar and cinnamon then cover and place over a medium heat to cook for 5 minutes. Remove the lid and stir the plums, then cook for another 3–4 minutes until they are soft through. Remove from the heat and set aside until cold.

Turn the cakes out onto a wire rack and leave to cool. When they are completely cold, whip the double cream until soft peaks form. Spoon the plums over one half of the cake, top with a layer of the whipped cream, then place the second cake on top. Dust with icing sugar before serving.

I'm sure you'll agree that this is one spectacular-looking cake. For the filling and decoration, I would always use fresh coconut rather than dried, as the latter tends to dry out the buttercream, but you could toast the coconut shavings first, if you like.

COCONUT CAKE

Serves 6–8

For the cake

50g coconut cream

50g coconut oil

175g butter, softened, plus extra for greasing

200g caster sugar

3 eggs

1 tsp vanilla extract

175g plain flour

2 tsp baking powder

50g desiccated coconut

For the buttercream

125g softened butter

40g coconut cream

250g icing sugar, sifted

50–75g coconut shavings

3–4 sprigs lemon verbena

Preheat the oven to 180°C/350°F/Gas mark 4. Grease and line two 17cm deep-sided cake tins.

Gently heat the coconut cream and oil together in a small saucepan until liquid, then set aside to cool slightly.

Put the butter and caster sugar into a kitchen mixer or large bowl and beat until lightened and fluffy. Add the eggs, one by one. Add the vanilla extract then sift in the flour and baking power and fold together. Add the desiccated coconut, cooled coconut cream and oil and mix well, then divide between the prepared cake tins.

Smooth the tops over and bake for about 20–25 minutes until golden brown and risen. A skewer inserted into the centre should come out clean – if it doesn't, return the cakes to the oven for another 5 minutes and repeat.

Cool on a wire rack for 15 minutes before turning out of the tins and cooling completely.

Meanwhile, make the buttercream. Beat the softened butter, coconut cream and icing sugar together in a food mixer or a bowl with an electric whisk until really light, fluffy and almost white in colour.

Spoon the icing into a piping bag fitted with a 13mm plain nozzle. Pipe swirls of coconut cream all over one sponge, then scatter some coconut shavings over the top, so that they stick out around the edge of the cake. Gently lay the second cake on top. Pipe small peaks of cream all over the top of the cake and finish with some more coconut shavings and small sprigs of lemon verbena.

This Spanish-influenced cake recipe really showcases honey, so use the very best you can get your hands on (though there's no point splashing out on manuka honey for this, as its benefits will be lost when it is cooked). Honey and almonds is a much-loved combination across Spain, appearing in both savoury and sweet dishes.

HONEY AND ALMOND CAKE
WITH HONEY GLAZE

Serves 8–10

For the cake

100g butter, plus extra for greasing

185g good-quality honey

3 eggs

300g ground almonds

200g crème fraîche

1½ tsp bicarbonate of soda

zest of 2 oranges

For the glaze

125g good-quality honey

200ml double cream

zest of 2 oranges

Crème Fraîche Sorbet (see page 45),
   to serve (optional)

Preheat the oven to 180°C/350°F/Gas mark 4. Grease and line a 23cm springform cake tin.

Heat the butter and honey in a saucepan until melted, then set aside to cool. Whisk the eggs and cooled honey mixture in a food mixer, or in a bowl with an electric whisk, until thickened and very light in colour. Working quickly so that the mixture stays light and airy, fold in the ground almonds, then fold in the crème fraîche, bicarbonate of soda and orange zest.

Spoon into the lined tin and bake in the oven for 30 minutes until risen and light golden brown. A skewer inserted into the centre of the cake should come out clean – if it doesn't, return the cake to the oven for a further 5 minutes and repeat.

Remove from the oven and cool on a wire rack for 10 minutes, then turn out the cake.

To make the glaze, place the honey and double cream in a saucepan, bring to the boil and simmer for a few minutes until the liquid thickens slightly. Add the orange zest. Spoon the honey glaze over the top of the cake and serve warm with a spoonful of Crème Fraîche Sorbet, if liked.

I first came across really good palmiers when I was working on the pastry section in a restaurant in the south of France. The trick is to get an even dusting of sugar, so that as the palmiers cook it caramelises to a nice glaze. Palmiers are often offered as a petit four to end a meal, but sandwiched with raspberries and cream, they're hard to beat for afternoon tea. These are best served at room temperature – once they go into the fridge, the butter in the pastry solidifies, making them less pleasant to eat.

BUTTERFLY PALMIERS WITH RASPBERRIES AND CREAM

Serves 6

650g puff pastry (see page 12), or good-quality, bought all-butter puff pastry

flour, for dusting

60g caster sugar

100ml stock syrup glaze (see page 29; optional)

For the filling

300ml double cream, softly whipped

200g raspberries

Preheat the oven to 180°C/350°F/Gas mark 4. Line 2 large baking sheets with silicone paper.

Roll the pastry out on a lightly floured surface to a rectangle 25cm x 40cm and about 3mm thick, with the long side facing you, like a landscape picture.

Dust the pastry rectangle with 20g of the caster sugar then fold one long side of the pastry into the centre. Repeat with the other long side to meet it, so you now have a piece half the width. Dust with another 20g of the caster sugar, then repeat, folding each side into the centre, leaving a 5mm gap in the centre. Dust once more with the remaining sugar and repeat – you should now have three folds on each side with plenty of sugar sandwiched in between. Fold both sides together gently as you would close an open book, then transfer to a tray and place in the freezer for 30 minutes to firm up.

Remove the roll and cut into 12 x 1cm-thick slices. Lay on a lined baking tray, spacing them so that they are at least 6cm apart. Bake for 12–15 minutes until golden and crispy.

Remove the palmiers from the oven, turn them straight over, place back on the tray and brush them with a little stock syrup glaze, if liked. The palmiers are best eaten on the day you make them.

When cold, spoon the whipped cream into a piping bag fitted with a 1cm nozzle and pipe the cream over half the palmiers. Top with some lightly crushed raspberries and another palmier. Serve immediately.

Over the years I've tried so many different gingerbread recipes from my grandmother and aunties – the same people who taught me how to bake properly in the first place – but this recipe comes from a French pastry chef I worked with here in the UK. Take my advice: once you have a trusted gingerbread recipe, tweak it to really make it your own, then stick with it. I think I've just about mastered the art of gingerbread after all this time…

GINGERBREAD BISCUITS

Makes about 20–25 biscuits

200g butter, softened

200g light brown soft sugar

4 tbsp golden syrup

1 tbsp treacle

1 tbsp water

500g plain flour, plus extra for dusting

¼ tsp bicarbonate of soda

1 tbsp ground ginger

2 tsp ground mixed spice

½ tsp ground cloves

royal icing (see page 41) and silver balls and sprinkles, to decorate

Beat the butter, sugar, golden syrup, treacle and water together in a food mixer, or in a bowl with an electric whisk, until very soft and light. Sift in the flour, bicarbonate of soda and spices. Mix everything together to form a soft dough.

Lightly flour a work surface, then knead the dough gently until smooth. Pat down until about 1cm thick then cover with clingfilm and place in the fridge to rest.

Preheat the oven to 180°C/350°F/Gas mark 4. Roll the dough out to about 3mm thick then stamp into star shapes and discs with cutters. Transfer to a lined baking sheet. Place in the oven and bake for 8–10 minutes until just starting to colour at the edges. Remove from the oven and allow the biscuits to cool and firm up on the baking sheet before removing.

Decorate the gingerbread with royal icing and silver balls and sprinkles, as you wish.

I love the intense ginger flavour of this simple cake, mellowed with orange and sweet spices. If you like, you could add some grated orange zest to the icing for extra zing, or try making the cake with rhubarb and ginger.

GINGER AND ORANGE CAKE

Serves 8–10

For the cake

150g butter, plus extra for greasing

200g light muscovado sugar

50g black treacle

200g golden syrup

50ml syrup from a jar of stem ginger

300ml whole milk

2 eggs

1 tsp vanilla extract

300g self-raising flour

1½ tsp bicarbonate of soda

2 tbsp ground ginger

1 tsp ground cinnamon

¼ tsp ground cloves

75g stem ginger, finely grated

zest of 1 orange

For the buttercream filling

160g butter, softened

100g icing sugar, sifted

zest of 1 orange

25g stem ginger, finely grated

For the icing

160g icing sugar

1–2 tbsp orange juice

25g stem ginger, finely grated

Preheat the oven to 170°C/325°F/Gas mark 3 and grease and line a 1kg loaf tin.

Put the butter, sugar, treacle and both syrups into a saucepan and heat gently until melted. Remove from the heat and allow to cool slightly before adding the milk, eggs and vanilla, then beat well until combined.

Sift the flour, bicarbonate of soda, ground ginger, cinnamon and cloves into a large bowl then pour in the melted-butter mixture and beat well. Add the stem ginger and orange zest and mix until combined, then pour into the prepared tin. Bake in the oven for 60 minutes until golden and risen. A skewer inserted into the centre of the cake should come out clean – if it doesn't, return to the oven for a further 5 minutes and repeat.

Cool on a wire rack for 5 minutes then tip out of the tin and return to the wire rack to cool completely.

While the cake cools, make the buttercream filling. Beat the softened butter and icing sugar together in a food mixer, or in a bowl with an electric whisk, until really light and fluffy – almost white in colour. Add the orange zest and grated stem ginger and mix to combine.

When the cake is cold, slice in half horizontally using a long, serrated knife and turning the cake as you go. Spread the buttercream over the base. Cover with the top half.

To make the icing, sieve the icing sugar into a bowl, add 1 tbsp orange juice and mix together to a thick paste. Add the grated stem ginger. Now add enough orange juice to make a spoonable icing and spread over the top of the cake. Leave to set before serving.

This is one of my favourite recipes in the book. I first came across monkey bread in the Dumbo ('Down Under the Manhattan Bridge') district of Brooklyn, a trendy part of New York, with modern apartments sprouting among old warehouses. I was staying with a couple who own a bakery, where they make this bread several times a day using their leftover doughnut dough. Eat this fresh from the oven with a cup of coffee, and you'll soon understand why they can barely keep up with the demand.

MONKEY BREAD

Serves 8–10

300ml milk

500g strong plain flour, plus extra
   for dusting

75g caster sugar

5g fine sea salt

50g butter, softened, plus extra
   for greasing

2 tsp fast-action dried yeast
   or 25g fresh yeast

200ml maple syrup

For the coating

250g demerara sugar

1 tbsp ground cinnamon

200g butter, melted

Place the milk in a saucepan and gently heat on the hob until warm to the finger.

To make the dough, put the flour into a large bowl or a kitchen mixer with a dough hook, add the sugar and salt and mix to combine. Add the softened butter and beat until it forms fine breadcrumbs, or rub together with your fingertips if not using a mixer. Add the yeast to the warm milk and mix everything together to form a soft dough.

If using a kitchen mixer, mix for 5 minutes on a medium speed until the dough is quite soft, sticky and shiny. If the dough is too dry at this stage, the bread will be dry when cooked; a tacky texture between your fingers is ideal.

If you're kneading the dough by hand, turn it out onto a floured surface and knead gently for about 5 minutes. Wash and dry your hands, then sprinkle the dough with a little more flour and continue to knead for a further 10 minutes until it is very pliable, smooth and slightly shiny – the dough should be slightly sticky, as above.

Place the dough in a large bowl and cover with clingfilm or a tea towel. Leave in a warm

place for 1–2 hours until well risen, spongy and nearly doubled in size.

Butter a 23cm savarin mould. Turn the dough out onto a lightly floured surface and knock it back with your knuckles. Knead for 1 minute then divide into 30–35 small, equal-sized balls.

Mix the demerara sugar and cinnamon together and set aside. Toss the balls of dough carefully, first in the melted butter and then in the sugar-and-cinnamon mixture. Place a layer of them into the buttered mould. Continue with all the balls until you have two layers. Cover loosely with oiled clingfilm and leave in a warm place for about 45 minutes, or until the dough is well risen.

Preheat the oven to 180°C/350°F/Gas mark 4. Bake for 25–30 minutes until golden brown. Drizzle the monkey bread with half the maple syrup before leaving it to cool in the tin for 2 minutes. Turn out onto a plate and drizzle with the rest of the maple syrup. You need to turn the bread out while it's still warm or it will stick to the mould.

You can fill these with whatever dried or fresh fruit you like, but a spoonful of the crème pâtissière in the Basics chapter will make all the difference to your Danishes, keeping them moist as they cook. You can also pipe a little icing over the top, if you like.

DANISH PASTRIES

Makes 30

2 quantities laminated enriched yeast dough (see page 26)

flour, for dusting

For the sultana whirls

2 eggs, beaten

100g caster sugar

150g sultanas

40g flaked almonds

butter, for greasing

100ml stock syrup glaze (see page 29)

For the fruit Danish

4 tbsp cherry pie filling

4 tinned pineapple rings, drained and patted dry

1 egg, beaten

4 tbsp good-quality lemon curd

100ml stock syrup glaze

For the sultana whirls, roll out one quantity of the dough on a lightly-floured surface, to a rectangle 25cm x 50cm and 7mm thick. Brush with the egg wash, then sprinkle over the sugar, sultanas and flaked almonds. Starting with the longest side, roll up loosely into a sausage. Cut into 18 pieces, about 3cm thick. Transfer to 2 lightly greased baking trays. Set aside to prove at room temperature, uncovered, for 30 minutes.

Preheat the oven to 200°C/400°F/Gas mark 6. Bake the pastries for 15–20 minutes until golden. Brush with the glaze whilst warm.

For the fruit Danish, roll out the second quantity of dough to a rectangle 30cm x 40cm and around 7mm thick. Divide into 12 squares, each 10cm x 10cm. Take 4 squares and, starting 1cm in from the corner, cut a line at a right angle, from the top-left to bottom-right corner, stopping short 1cm in from the bottom-right corner. Fold the bottom-left corner into the centre then fold the top-right corner over to form a diamond. Fill with a tablespoon of cherry pie filling. Transfer to a lightly greased baking tray. Leave to prove at room temperature, uncovered, for 30 minutes.

Take another 4 squares and cut an L-shape in the corners of each, about 1cm in from the edge, so the right-angle lines are parallel to the outside edges. Extend the lines to follow the edges of the squares but stop short so there is 1cm of uncut dough at the centre of each side. Brush each corner with egg wash then place the pineapple ring in the centre. Fold the edges in over the pineapple to partly cover, then press down gently on the centre pieces to secure. Transfer to a lightly greased baking tray. Leave to prove at room temperature, uncovered, for 30 minutes.

Brush the last 4 squares with egg wash. Pipe a tablespoon of lemon curd diagonally across the centre, leaving a 1.5cm gap at either end. Pull the sides out to stretch them gently, then fold one over the top of the lemon curd, then the other over this. Wrap underneath to secure. Transfer to a lightly greased baking tray then leave to prove at room temperature, uncovered, for 30–40 minutes.

Bake at 200°C/400°F/Gas mark 6 for about 20–25 minutes until golden and slightly crisp. Brush with the stock syrup glaze whilst warm, then leave to cool slightly before serving.

TROUBLESHOOTING

This is just as important as the recipes in this book. When things go wrong – and they will – you need to know what happens and why it happens, so you can move forward with your cooking. I hope these tips and information come in useful.

PASTRY

Pastry is hard and tough, either before or after baking
* Too much flour has been used to dust the worksurface
* Too much liquid has been used in making the pastry (usually water)
* The pastry has been overmixed or overhandled
* The oven temperature was too low
* Not enough butter or fat has been used
* There is too much sugar in the pastry

Pastry is too short
* Not enough liquid (egg or water) was used in the pastry
* The fat was not rubbed in well enough, or the lumps of fat were too large
* The pastry was not mixed well enough
* There is too much fat in the pastry

Pastry shrinks when baked
* The pastry was not rested before baking
* The pastry was overworked during mixing or rolling out
* The pastry was overstretched during shaping
* The oven temperature was too low

PUFF PASTRY

Pastry does not rise properly when baked
* The oven is not hot enough (the butter is melting but not creating steam)
* The flour used was of poor quality
* The butter or fat was not cold enough when laminating
* The pastry was rolled too thinly when laminating
* The pastry was given too many turns, resulting in overworking
* The pastry was not cleanly cut with sharp lines during shaping

The pastry shrinks when baked
* The pastry was not left to rest after 'pinning out'
* The pastry was not left to rest before baking

Butter is visible in lumps through the unbaked pastry
* The butter was too cold when it was folded into the pastry
* The pastry was not rested for long enough between turns

CAKES

'Sad' streak or dense layer under top crust
* Cake was not baked for long enough
* Cake was moved or knocked during baking
* The oven was too hot

'Sad' streak or dense layer at bottom of cake
* Not enough baking powder was used
* Not enough sugar was used
* Not enough egg was used
* Too much liquid was used
* The flour used was not 'strong' enough

Centre of cake has collapsed, white spots on crust
* Too much sugar was used

Centre of cake has collapsed, cake has dark crust
* Too much baking powder was used

Cake is small, with 'cauliflower' top
* Not enough sugar was used
* Too much egg was used
* Oven was too hot
* The flour used was of poor quality

Cake has long holes in crumb
* Not enough air was introduced during mixing
* Butter and sugar were not 'creamed' for long enough
* Batter was overmixed after the flour had been added

Cake has discoloured crumb
* Too much baking powder was used

Cake has crumb that's too tender
* Too much fat was used, in relation to egg

Cake has crumb with coarse, open texture
* Not enough fat was used in relation to egg
* Too much sugar was used
* Too much baking powder was used
* The flour used was of poor quality
* The oven was too cool and the cake baked too slowly

Fruit has sunk to bottom of cake
* Not enough flour was used, or the flour was of poor quality
* Not enough egg was used
* Too much baking powder was used
* Too much sugar was used
* Mixing was too light or insufficient, batter was overcreamed
* The oven was too cool and the cake baked too slowly
* The fruit was too heavy; fruit was wet; syrup not washed off fruit

EGG-SUGAR SPONGES

Sponge sinks in middle when baked
* Oven was opened during baking, causing a sudden drop in temperature
* Not enough flour was used
* Too much sugar was used

Sponge is dense and does not rise well
* Eggs and sugar were underwhisked
* Batter was overworked when the flour was folded in
* Oven temperature was too low
* Too much butter was added

Sponge is uneven when baked
* Tin was poorly greased and floured
* Temperature of oven was uneven

EQUIPMENT AND SUPPLIERS

CHOCOLATE TRADING COMPANY

www.chocolatetradingco.com; 01625 508224

For all types of fine chocolate

COUNTRY PRODUCTS

www.countryproducts.co.uk; 01423 358858

For glacé fruits and other specialist ingredients

THE CRAFT COMPANY

www.craftcompany.co.uk; 01926 888507

For cake decorations and cake-decorating equipment

DENBY RETAIL LTD

www.denby.co.uk; 01773 740899

For dinnerware, glassware, cookware and pans

FINE FOOD SPECIALIST

www.finefoodspecialist.co.uk; 0845 272 5916

For specialist ingredients and produce

HORWOOD HOMEWARES LTD

www.horwood.co.uk; www.stellar.co.uk; 0117 940 0000

For Horwood and Stellar cookware and bakeware

KOPPERT CRESS BV

www.greatbritain.koppertcress.com; 00 31 174 24 28 19

For micro herbs, cress and baby leaves

LAKELAND

www.lakeland.co.uk; 015394 88100

For all kinds of baking and kitchen equipment

MSK SPECIALIST INGREDIENTS

www.msk-ingredients.com; 01246 412211

For ultratex and other specialist ingredients

NISBETS

www.nisbets.co.uk; 0845 140 5555

For all baking and kitchen essentials, espuma guns and cartridges, plus electrical appliances

SUGARSHACK

www.sugarshack.co.uk; 020 8204 2994

For all kinds of cake tins and baking equipment

WAHL

www.wahlstore.co.uk; 01227 740066

For food processors, blenders, scales and other kitchen equipment

INDEX

Acknowledgements

Just as this book is launched, I'll be celebrating 20 years in front of the television cameras, and everything I've learnt over the years has gone into these pages. To my mind, this is the best book I have done to date – with the help of so many people, though. First off, my right hand and left hand, Chris Start and Pippa Bull: thank you, you two, for keeping me busy and focussed. Thanks also to Janet and the team at Quadrille, for pressing me to get it done, and for making sure all my madness makes some sort of sense. To Peter Cassidy, for your amazing work taking the pictures: you really are a genius, and I'm sure we'll be working together many more times as we both hate blurry pics. And finally to my mother, sis, Pete and Louise, for keeping me on the straight and narrow all these years, and for looking after the real tasters of this book, Ralph and Fudge, while I'm away.